IELTS
Practice
Tests ▶ Plus

Vanessa Jakeman
Clare McDowell

Longman

CONTENTS

INTRODUCTION TO IELTS

IELTS stands for *International English Language Testing System*. It is a test of English language skills designed for students who want to study in the medium of English either at university, college or secondary school.

There are two versions of the test: the **Academic Module** and the **General Training (GT) Module**. Students wishing to study at postgraduate or undergraduate level should take the Academic Module. The General Training Module is designed for those candidates who plan to undertake training or secondary school education. The General Training Module is also used in Australia and New Zealand to assess the language skills of incoming migrants. Candidates must decide in advance which of the two modules they wish to sit as the results are not interchangeable.

Students sit the Listening, Reading and Writing papers in that order on one day. The Speaking Test may be held up to two days later, though normally it is taken on the same day, after the Writing Test.

A computerised version of the Listening, Reading and Writing Tests will be available at some IELTS centres but the paper-based version of IELTS will always be offered and is the standard format.

Overview of the test

The test is in four parts reflecting the four basic language skills:

- **Listening** *taken by all candidates*
- **Reading** *Academic or General Training*
- **Writing** *Academic or General Training*
- **Speaking** *taken by all candidates*

Results

Performance is rated on a scale of 1–9. Candidates receive a Test Report Form which shows their overall performance reported as a single band score as well as the individual scores they received for each part of the test.

OVERVIEW OF THE IELTS TEST

Listening	No. of items	Discourse types	No. of speakers	Question types	Target Listening Skills
Played once only Total 30 mins	**40**				**Listening for**
Section 1	10	A dialogue – social or transactional.	2	• short answer. • multiple choice.	• specific information.
Section 2	10	A talk or short speech – topic of general interest.	1	• sentence completion.	• main ideas and supporting points.
Section 3	10	A conversation – education/training context.	2 – 4	• notes/summary/diagram flow chart/table completion.	• understanding speakers' opinion.
Section 4	10	A lecture – academic style.	1	• matching. • classification.	

Academic Reading	No of items	Text types	Question types	Target Reading Skills
60 mins	**40**	**Total of 2,000 – 2,750 words**	**Up to 4 per passage**	
Passage 1	13–14	Academic texts – ie journals, newspapers, text books and magazines representative of reading. requirements for postgraduate and undergraduate students. General interest rather than discipline specific. Graded in difficulty.	• paragraph headings. • short answers. • multiple choice. • sentence completion. • notes/summary/diagram/ flow chart/table completion. • matching lists/phrases. • classification. • identification of writer's views/claims. • Yes, No, Not Given • True, False, Not Given	• scanning & skimming. • understanding main ideas. • reading for detail. • understanding opinion and attitude.
Passage 2	13–14			
Passage 3	13–14			

Academic Writing	No. of tasks	Text types	Task types	Target Writing Skills
60 mins	**2**			
Task 1 (20 mins)	150 words	A descriptive report based on graphic or pictorial input.	Information transfer exercise (No analysis required).	• present, describe, interpret, compare given data. • describe a process or how something works. • use appropriate and accurate language.
Task 2 (40 mins)	250 words	An extended piece of writing or discursive essay.	Candidates are presented with a given point of view or problem on which to base their writing.	• argue, defend or attack a point of view backed by evidence. • present the solution to a problem. • compare & contrast opinions drawing on personal experience.

General Training Reading	No of items	Discourse types	Question types	Target Reading Skills
60 mins	**40**	**Total of 2,000 – 2,750 words**	**Up to 4 per part**	
Section 1 Social Survival	13–14	Social or transactional texts taken from everyday situations. Up to 3 texts are possible.	• paragraph headings. • short answers. • multiple choice. • sentence completion. • notes/summary/diagram/ flow chart/table completion. • matching lists/phrases. • True, False, Not Given. • classification. • identification of writer's views/claims. • Yes, No, Not Given.	• scanning & skimming. • understanding main ideas. • reading for detail. • understanding opinion and attitude. • inferring meaning.
Section 2 Course Related	13–14	Course related texts drawn from an educational or training context but focusing on survival needs of students.		
Section 3 General Reading	13–14	Descriptive or narrative text of extended prose on a topic of general interest.		

General Training Writing	No of tasks	Writing types	Task types	Target Writing Skills
60 mins	**2**			
Task 1 (20 mins)	150 words	A short letter – informal or semi formal style.	Task poses a problem or outlines a situation which requires a written response in letter format.	• respond to task. • show familiarity with letter writing style. • use appropriate and accurate language.
Task 2 (40 mins)	250 words	Discursive essay.	An extended piece of writing based on a number of points raised in the question.	• express a point of view on the topic. • present an opinion backed by evidence. • compare & contrast opinions drawing on personal experience.

INTRODUCTION

Speaking	No. of parts	Format 1:1	Nature of interaction	Target Speaking Skills
11–14 mins	3	Examiner & candidate		
Part 1	4–5 mins	Introduction & interview.	Examiner interviews candidate asking questions based on familiar topics, using a set framework.	• giving personal information. • talking about familiar issues and habits. • expressing opinions.
Part 2	3–4 mins	Individual long turn.	Candidate is required to speak for 1–2 minutes on a topic presented in the form of both a written and verbal instruction. Candidate is given 1 minute to prepare.	• sustaining a long turn without interlocutor support. • managing language: organisation and expression of ideas.
Part 3	4–5 mins	Discussion.	Examiner introduces a discussion thematically linked to the Part 2 topic and encourages the candidate to develop language of a more abstract and academic nature.	• expressing and justifying views. • explaining. • displaying understanding of the conversational rules of English.

The Speaking test format in brief

Part 1 – you will be asked some questions based on everyday topics and your personal experiences. You should answer these as fully as possible without straying from the topic.

Part 2 – you will have to speak for between one and two minutes on a topic nominated by the examiner. You will have a minute to prepare but then you must speak without stopping.

Part 3 – you will be asked to speak on issues broadly related to the Part 2 topic. The examiner will lead the discussion but you are expected to interact fully and offer a broad range of language appropriate to the subject and situation.

SKILLS FOR IELTS

LISTENING SKILLS

The IELTS examination tests your ability to understand spoken language in a variety of social and academic contexts. The test consists of four graded recorded sections each with 10 questions and it takes about 30 minutes to complete. As you hear the recording **once** only, success will depend on knowing what information to listen for. You are not expected to have any specialist knowledge but you should be able to deal with a range of topics and a number of different voices.

The test measures how well you can manage the following skills:

▶ Listening for specific information

▶ Listening for main ideas and supporting information

▶ Understanding the speaker's opinion

Each of the four sections in the listening test may have up to three different types of question testing a range of skills.

<table>
<tr><td>

Developing listening skills 1

</td><td>

Listening for specific information

</td></tr>
</table>

▶ **What does 'listening for specific information' mean?**

When you listen for specific information, you are listening for key details; for example, to help you make a decision or complete a task.

Exercise 1 ▷ *Imagine you are listening to the following. What kind of information might you want to listen for in each case?*

Example: a radio advert for a mobile phone: *price, name of store, accessories*

1 the weather forecast
2 a radio sports bulletin

3 a news item about a storm
4 a recorded message at a cinema

▶ **How is your ability to listen for specific information tested in IELTS?**

In the exam, you may need to show your understanding of specific information by:

• filling in gaps in a set of notes or summary

• completing a form

• answering multiple choice questions

• writing short answers to questions

• completing a grid or chart

• picking words from a list.

Exercise 2 ▷ **a** 📼 *Read the questions below and decide what type of information you need to listen out for. Will you need to write something or choose an answer?*

*Now listen to **Extracts 1 and 2** and answer Questions 1, 2 and 3.*

Concert details

Full price tickets*:*　　　　　$35.00

Student price: **1** ....

Concert begins at: **2** ....

3　When does the man want to start the English course?

　　A　March

　　B　April

　　C　September

---

b 📼 *Look at Questions 4, 5 and 6 in the box below. Underline the key words in each question, that is, the words which tell you what information to listen out for. For example, the key word in Question 4 is 'work', so you need to listen for what job the man does.*

*Now listen to **Extract 3** and answer questions 4–6.*

Exam Tip

The words you need are on the recording. Remember, you cannot use more than three words in a short answer question.

4　What kind of work does the man do?　........................

5　What product does the man ask about?　........................

6　What item does the man give the woman?　........................

Exercise 3 ▷ **a** *Look at the statements and possible answers below. Turn them into questions by changing the stem. The first one is done for you.*

1 The library opens at
A 9.00a.m.
B 10.00a.m.
C 11.00a.m.

What time does the library open?

2 The police arrived by
A　car.
B　motor bike.
C　helicopter.

3 The graph shows the

    A number of people in prison in Australia.

    B main reason for people going to prison.

    C number of prisons in Australia.

4 Louis Braille was born in

    A 1809.

    B 1819.

    C 1829.

b ▢ *Now listen to **Extract 3** again and answer Questions 7 and 8.*

Exam Tip

You are not always listening for the words used in the question. IELTS tests your ability to make sense of what you hear – not just to listen for key words. Sometimes one of the speakers will ask the question for you in a slightly different form so listen out for this.

7 The woman washes her hair

    A once a week.

    B twice a week.

    C more than twice a week.

8 The woman chooses her shampoo based on

    A price.

    B design.

    C advertising.

How was the answer expressed on the recording? Were the same words used as in the question?

Developing listening skills 2

Listening for main ideas and supporting information

▶ **What does 'listening for main ideas' mean?**

Imagine you are at a party. You join a group of people who are already talking to each other. The first thing you do is try to work out what they are talking about. What is the topic? And then, what is the main idea? You can get an idea of the topic from the vocabulary they are using. The main idea is the main point or message.

Exercise 4 ▷ **a** ▢ *Listen to **Extract 4**. You will hear four different mini-talks; in each case identify the main idea and complete the table below. Sometimes the main idea will be explicitly stated, sometimes it will be in the overall message.*

b ▢ *Listen to **Extract 4** again and pause the recording after each speaker. Make notes of some of the supporting information. Look at the example for the first mini-talk below.*

	Main Ideas	Supporting Information
1	the cost of the project	$43 million since 1990
2		
3		
4		

▶ **How is your understanding of main ideas and supporting information tested in the IELTS exam?**

In the exam, you may need to show your understanding of main ideas and supporting information by:

- answering short questions
- answering multiple choice questions
- filling in gaps in a set of notes
- choosing a word from a list
- completing a diagram, a chart or a grid
- summary completion.

Exercise 5 ▷ **a** 📼 *Read Question 9. Is this question testing main ideas or supporting information? Now listen to **Extract 5** and answer the question.*

Exam Tip

When information is deliberately repeated in an IELTS listening, it may be the information you need. How often did the speaker repeat the main idea?

> *Answer the questions using NO MORE THAN THREE WORDS.*
>
> **9** What is the subject of the man's talk? ....

b 📼 *Another task that tests your understanding of main ideas is multiple choice. For example, in Question 10 below, you must decide which of the 3 options best sums up what the man says. Listen to **Extract 6** and answer the question.*

> *Circle the appropriate letter A–C*
>
> **10** The shoes were designed to …
>
> **A** reduce the pain of marathon running.
>
> **B** increase the athletes' speed.
>
> **C** help old people walk more easily.

Exercise 6 ▷ **a** *The IELTS may use summary completion to test your understanding of supporting details. The words in the summary will give a brief version of what you hear. Read the summary below. What is the main idea? Underline the words that tell you. What details do you need?*

*Now listen to **Extract 7** and answer Questions 11–14.*

> *Complete the summary using NO MORE THAN THREE WORDS or A NUMBER for each answer.*
>
> ### The Flagship of the Royal Fleet
>
> The *Mary Rose* sank in the year **11** .... The king stood on the shore and watched her go down. The ship then lay on the sea bed for **12** .... years. In 1982 she was **13** .... and brought back to dry land. By analysing the **14** .... of the ship, scientists believe they are closer to learning why she sank.

▶▶ Now go to Test 3, Questions 36–40, and try a summary completion task.

b 🔲 *Another way of testing your understanding of supporting detail is selecting from a list. Listen to **Extract** 8 and answer Question 15 below.*

Exam Tip

You have to get both answers correct to get your mark.

*Circle **TWO** letters A–G.*

15 Which **TWO** of the following items must the girl take with her?

A hiking boots	**E** gloves
B pair of shorts	**F** tent
C woollen jumper	**G** flashlight
D inflatable mattress	

Developing listening skills 3

Understanding the speaker's opinion

▶ **How can you tell opinions from facts?**

An opinion is a point of view; it differs from a fact in that it cannot be proved true. Some people make their opinions sound like facts, but usually when people give a verbal opinion, they use phrases such as *'I believe, I think, In my opinion …'*.

Exercise 7 ▷ *Which of the following are opinions? Which are facts? How do you know?*

1 As far as I can see, the increase in petrol prices is due to the government's taxation policy.

2 These days all children can be immunised against diseases such as measles and mumps. Here's a leaflet with the information you require.

3 I'm sure that if children aren't taught how to socialise when they are young, they will have difficulty getting on with other adults later on in life.

4 The law forbids people from driving faster than 70km an hour in most parts of the city.

▶ **How is understanding speaker's opinion tested in the IELTS Listening Module?**

Opinion is usually only tested in Sections 3 and 4 of the listening test. The most common method is through multiple-choice questions as these can provide you with a choice of opinions from which to select the correct answer.

Exercise 8 ▷ 🔲 *Look at Questions 16–17 below. Are you listening for an opinion or a fact? Which words tell you? Listen to **Extracts 9–10** and answer the questions.*

16 The student thinks that the building

 A is very cleverly designed.

 B is adequate for its purpose.

 C has a number of design faults.

17 What is the speaker's view of bicycles?

 A They will not change much in the future.

 B They should be designed to be more practical.

 C They can cover greater distances than in the past.

▶▶ Now go to Test 1, Quetsions 8–9, and try a selecting task.

Good reading skills are vital for academic studies. The IELTS exam tests your ability to use a variety of reading skills. You have one hour to answer questions on three reading passages, so it is important to identify which skills are being tested in each question and to apply them appropriately.

The main reading skills tested in IELTS are:

▶ scanning

▶ skimming

▶ understanding main ideas

▶ reading for detail

▶ understanding opinions

Developing reading skills 1

Skimming and scanning

▶ **What is skimming?**

Skimming means **reading very quickly**. It involves selective reading of the most important parts of the text in order to:

- find out how the text is organised – that is, the way it is divided into sections or paragraphs
- get a general idea of what the text is about.

The way in which a text is organised gives us a clue as to what is the most important part to read.

Exercise 1 ▷ *Tick what you should read to get a quick overview of a text. The first one is done for you.*

a) the title and sub-heading ✓

b) the introduction ____

c) every part of the text ____

d) the first and last sentences of each paragraph in the main body ____

e) the conclusion ____

f) the middle of each paragraph ____

▶ **What is scanning?**

When you scan a text, you move your eyes over it very quickly in order to find something specific and easily recognisable. When scanning you are looking for particular information (e.g. names, places, dates, specific phrases).

Exercise 2 ▷ *Which of these types of text would you scan? Which would you skim? Tick the appropriate box:*

	Skim	Scan
a phone book	☐	☐
a newspaper article you are interested in	☐	☐
the film review page when looking for a particular film	☐	☐
a letter from the bank	☐	☐
a list of results for an exam you've taken	☐	☐

► **How are skimming and scanning useful for IELTS?**

Skimming and scanning are 'enabling skills'. This means that they help you tackle most questions in the exam more effectively, including for example:

- multiple choice questions
- matching opinions and phrases
- completing a table
- labelling a diagram.

Exercise 3 ▷ **a** *The text below has been edited to highlight the areas that you might read when skimming or scanning a text. Read through it quickly and answer the following multiple-choice questions.*

Goodness, gracious, great balls of fire

In the first of a new series, Alan Watts tackles the science of thunder and lightning

A Despite our modern sophistication and advanced warning systems, the thunderstorm still provokes a primitive dread in most people. It is not only our helplessness in the face of nature's wrath that produces fear, but also the eerie listlessness that settles over animals, birds and people in the build-up to a storm. Yet the kind of storm with a sultry calm before its arrival is just one of many kinds of thunderstorm associated with a particular kind of weather.

B The kinds of intense storms that develop on hot sultry days are a mass of individual storm cells.

'cell-theory' of storms .... 'multicell' .... 'supercell' .... multicell .... daughter-cells ....

C Then in spring, when the sun is warming the earth but the air is still cool, great towering *cumulonimbus* clouds often develop and these can become thundery.

.... 'air-mass' .... thunderstorms France .... English Channel ....

D If you've lived in the coastal regions of southern Britain, then you'll be acquainted with a special kind of storm that comes up from France a couple of times a year.

....

Spanish plume storms   sierras of Spain 'sheet-lightning'...............................

....

E Whatever the cause of a storm, there has to be lightning ....
pressure waves ....electric charge ......

raindrops ....positively charged ......
........................slivers of ice ....

F It is estimated that there are some 1,800 storms going on at any one time somewhere in the world—mainly in the tropics—and that the electric current induced by the lightning from these compensates for the more-or-less continuous drift of positive ions from the ionosphere to the earth, so balancing the atmosphere's electric current.

> **1** What is the article about?
>
> **A** fire
>
> **B** weather
>
> **C** science
>
> **2** Which of the following areas do you think the writer will discuss?
>
> **A** animals and their environment
>
> **B** modern danger warnings
>
> **C** types of storm
>
> **D** what to do in bad weather

b *Selective reading will also help you to orient yourself within a text. Look at the text on page 14. Which paragraphs will you need to read more carefully if you need to find out more about:*

1 the causes of lightning?

2 spring storms?

3 storms in particular regions of Europe?

4 storm cells?

Exercise 4 ▷ *The following questions form an IELTS task for the text on thunderstorms. The task is matching descriptions. For matching questions, the first step is to read the list of options and to locate the part of the text with the answer. In order to do this effectively, skimming and scanning are vital.*

Read the task and underline the words which you could scan the text for.

Exam Tip

Before you begin any set of questions always check to see whether you can use your skimming or scanning skills to help you locate the answer. Often you need to use both.

> *Look at the descriptions of thunderstorms below. Which type of storm (**A–C**) does each feature 1–6 refer to?*
>
> **A** Supercell or multicell storms
>
> **B** Air-mass storms
>
> **C** Spanish Plume storms
>
> **3** Which type of thunderstorm
>
> 1 can occur throughout the year?
>
> 2 is connected with certain physical land features?
>
> 3 features clouds at high and low altitudes?
>
> 4 is perpetuated by cyclical air currents?
>
> 5 is the most typical?
>
> 6 is intensified by the meeting of hot and cold air?

▶▶ Now go to Test 1, Questions 9–13, on page 39 and try a matching task.

Main ideas and details

▶ **How are texts organised?**

Texts are divided into paragraphs to make them easier to read. Usually a text is organised in the following way:

Introduction (para 1):	statement of theme
Paragraph 2:	supporting point
	details
Paragraph 3:	supporting point
	details
Etc.	
Conclusion:	summary and re-statement of main idea.

In the introduction the writer will outline what he or she will write about and the main issues he or she intends to raise.

Each paragraph goes on to deal with **one** key issue. The writer may state the issue in a topic sentence or sentences and may summarise it in the last sentence. The writer will use supporting details to explain and develop the point the paragraph is making. Sometimes the point has to be inferred from the details.

Exercise 5 ▷ *Read the following paragraph. Choose the main idea **A**, **B** or **C**. If there is a topic sentence, underline it.*

When philosophers debate what it is that makes humans unique among animals, they often point to language. Other animals can communicate, of course. But despite the best efforts of biologists working with beasts as diverse as chimpanzees, dolphins and parrots, no other species has yet shown the subtleties of syntax that give human languages their power. There is, however, another sonic medium that might be thought uniquely human and that is music. Other species can sing (indeed, many birds do so better than a lot of people) but birdsong and the song of animals such as whales, has a limited repertoire – and no other animal is known to have developed a musical instrument.

A the differences between animals and humans
B the characteristics of language and music
C the importance of language to humans

▶ **How is your understanding of main ideas tested in IELTS?**

In the IELTS exam you will need to show your understanding of main ideas by matching headings to paragraphs in a text.

Exercise 6 ▷ *Read the following instructions for a paragraph heading task.*

*Reading Passage 2 has seven paragraphs (**A–G**).*

From the list of headings below choose the most suitable heading for each paragraph.

*Write the appropriate numbers **i–x** in boxes 14–20 on your answer sheet.*

In which order will you follow these steps so that you can match the correct heading to each paragraph?

a) look for the topic sentences ☐   c) read through the list of headings ☐

b) select the right heading ☐   d) skim the whole text ☐

▶▶ Now try a paragraph heading task in Test 1, Questions 27–33, page 44.

▶ **What are details?**

A detail is an 'important' or 'specific' piece of information that can be found in a text. Details are often facts and in academic texts these are used to support main arguments.

Exercise 7 ▷ *Read the following sentences. Which one is the main idea? Which ones are details that support the main idea?*

a) Prices are stable.   c) Consumer confidence is up.

b) The economy is booming.   d) Interest rates are low.

Exam Tip

Some questions may test a mixture of skills. For example, a multiple choice task may test your understanding of main ideas and details.

▶ **How is your understanding of detail tested in IELTS?**

A number of different types of questions may test how well you can locate and understand detailed information. For example:

• sentence completion   • short answer questions

• multiple choice   • summary completion

Exercise 8 ▷ *In the summary completion task, you have to locate the ideas in the text and then select the **correct** words to complete the detailed information in the gaps.*

The following instructions come before a summary completion task.

> *Complete the summary below. Choose **NO MORE THAN THREE WORDS** from the passage for each answer.*
>
> *Write your answers in boxes 1–7 on your answer sheet.*

a *In what order will you follow these steps so that you can complete the summary completion task?*

a) predict the missing words ☐

b) read through the summary ☐

c) select the best word for each gap ☐

d) skim the passage in order to locate the area being tested in the summary ☐

e) read around each gap in the summary ☐

f) check the instructions ☐

Exam Tip

A summary completion task may also test your understanding of main ideas. This happens if the summary covers the whole text or a large part of the text.

b *Now complete the short summary below using words from the paragraph on the causes of storms.*

> Whatever the cause of a storm, there has to be lightning. You cannot have thunder without lightning because thunder is the sound of outspreading pressure waves from the sudden heating of the air along a lightning flash. How storms develop such immense amounts of electric charge is still not fully understood, but the most likely way is by raindrops carried skywards in updraughts in the clouds. As they are lifted into the higher, colder, regions they freeze on the outside. The shell of ice compresses the water inside it to the point at which it eventually bursts out and instantly freezes into positively charged slivers of ice.

> Scientists are still unsure how the … **1** …is produced during storms but they suspect that it is the result of … **2** … reaching the lower clouds and then … **3** … as it travels further upwards.

▶▶ Now try a summary completion task in Test 1, Questions 1–8, on page 38.

Exercise 9 ▷ *Unlike the paragraph headings task which focuses on main ideas, the paragraph matching task requires you to identify specific information within paragraphs. Each question paraphrases the information.*

Read the instructions for a paragraph matching task.

> *Reading Passage 2 has seven paragraphs A–G.*
> *Which paragraph mentions the following (Questions 14–21)?*
> *Write the appropriate letters (A–G) in boxes 14–21 on your answer sheet.*
> *NB Some of the paragraphs will be used more than once.*

In what order will you follow these steps in order to do the paragraph matching task?

a) select the questions that have key words that are easy to scan for ☐

b) read the whole passage quickly ☐

c) attempt the more difficult questions ☐

d) skim the passage for an idea that is
similar to the idea presented in the question ☐

e) note any key words or main ideas within the paragraphs ☐

f) read through the questions and underline the key words ☐

▶▶ Now try a paragraph matching task in Test 2, Questions 14–21, on page 64.

Understanding opinions

▶ **How do opinions differ from facts?**

An opinion is someone's 'belief' or 'view'. Opinions differ from facts in that they are open to debate and cannot be proved to be true. They may also change over time.

Exercise 10 ▷ *Which of the following statements are opinions?*

a) Computers have had a negative impact on children's reading habits.

b) Equatorial regions of the Earth have warm climates.

c) Medical treatment has improved over the past century.

▶ **How is your understanding of opinion tested in the IELTS Reading Module?**

As IELTS passages are academic texts, they usually contain arguments and opinions. Sometimes a passage presents the writer's opinions on a subject; sometimes a passage presents the views of the writer and other experts.

A number of different questions may test how well you can identify opinions including, for example:

• matching questions

• multiple choice questions

• YES, NO, NOT GIVEN questions.

Exercise 11 ▷ *Read the instructions for a YES, NO, NOT GIVEN task:*

> *Do the following statements agree with the views of the writer in Reading Passage 3?*
>
> *In boxes 32–37 on your answer sheet write*
>
> | | |
> |---|---|
> | *YES* | *if the statement agrees with the writer* |
> | *NO* | *if the statement contradicts the writer* |
> | *NOT GIVEN* | *if it is impossible to say what the writer thinks about this* |

The statements are a list of opinions. You will need to use a variety of reading skills to locate the area of the passage that the question focuses on. You will then need to decide whether the answer is:

YES = the writer holds the same opinion

NO = the writer holds the opposite opinion

NOT GIVEN = the writer does not say anything about this

Write YES, NO or NOT GIVEN next to the views of the writer, which are based on the paragraphs below.

Music is clearly different from language. People can, nevertheless, use it to communicate things – especially their emotions – and when allied with speech in a song, it is one of the most powerful means of communication that humans have. But what, biologically speaking, is it? If music is truly distinct from speech, then it ought to have a distinct processing mechanism in the brain – one that keeps it separate from the interpretation of other sounds, including language. The evidence suggests that such a separate mechanism does, indeed, exist.

Scientific curiosity about the auditory system dates back to the mid-19th century. In 1861 Paul Broca, a French surgeon, observed that speech was impaired by damage to a particular part of the brain, now known as Broca's area. In 1874 Carl Wernicke, a German neurologist, made a similar observation about another brain area and was similarly immortalised. The location of different language-processing tasks in Broca's areas (found in the brain's left temporal lobe, above the ear) was one of the first pieces of evidence that different bits of the brain are specialised to do different jobs.

a) Music needs words in order to become a truly effective means of communication.

b) Scientists are still looking for a way to show that the brain processes music and language separately.

c) Paul Broca attempted to distinguish the processing mechanisms of music and language.

d) The work of Broca and Wernicke marked the beginning of research into the brain and its role in the production of language.

▶▶ Follow the guidelines in the Tip Strip on page 42 when you do YES, NO, NOT GIVEN questions.

When you study in an academic context, you need to be able to write clear, formal English. There are two writing tasks in IELTS, reflecting some of the different types of writing that you will have to produce if you study in the medium of English. You have one hour to complete the two tasks. You will need to:

▶ complete the task appropriately

▶ organise and link your ideas clearly

▶ write accurately and with a good range of vocabulary

Developing writing skills 1

▶

Completing the task appropriately

▶ What is expected of you in Task 1?

In the IELTS Task 1, you may need to describe any of the following types of graphs or diagrams:

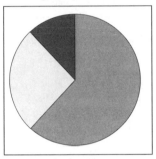
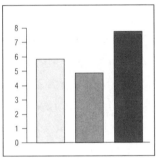
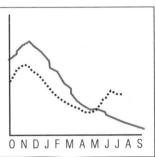

You may also have to describe a process illustrated by a diagram, or information presented in a table.

In answering a Task 1 question, you will need to:

• interpret the data accurately

• point out overall trends rather than details

• include only relevant information

• use appropriate vocabulary.

Exercise 1 ▷ **a** *Read the following task and answer these questions by referring to the graph on page 22:*

1 According to the instructions, what does the graph show?

2 What does OECD stand for? What do the numbers represent?

3 What is a key feature of the graph?

4 What trends are shown on the graph?

The graph below shows carbon dioxide emission in several areas of the world.

Write a report for a university lecturer describing the information shown below.

You should write at least 150 words.

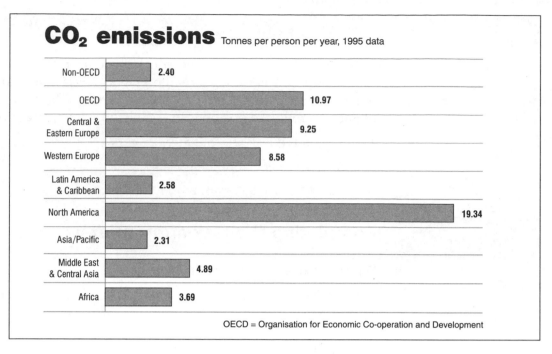

CO₂ emissions Tonnes per person per year, 1995 data

Region	Tonnes
Non-OECD	2.40
OECD	10.97
Central & Eastern Europe	9.25
Western Europe	8.58
Latin America & Caribbean	2.58
North America	19.34
Asia/Pacific	2.31
Middle East & Central Asia	4.89
Africa	3.69

OECD = Organisation for Economic Co-operation and Development

b *Read this sample description and answer the following questions.*

1 What information has the writer started with?
2 Are the figures correct?
3 What trends have been described?
4 How have the ideas been linked?

The graph shows that countries in the developed world produce far more CO_2 than developing countries. Not surprisingly, North America is the chief culprit producing 19.34 tonnes of CO_2 per person per year. This is almost double all the OECD countries combined. In contrast to this, Latin America and the Caribbean produce the smallest levels of CO_2 emission at 2.58 tonnes per person per year. European nations also emit huge amounts of CO_2, with Central and Eastern Europe producing 9.25 tonnes per capita, and Western Europe slightly less. However, this figure is still only half the North American statistic. Countries in Africa and the Asia/Pacific area, on the other hand, are only responsible for considerably smaller amounts.

▶▶ Now go to Test 1, and try the first writing task.
Refer to the **Tip Strip** in Test 1 for guidelines on how to approach Task 1.

▶ **What is expected of you in Task 2?**

In Task 2 you are expected to produce an academic style essay in which you present your views on the topic given. In order to do this you will have to follow the conventions of essay writing. You will need to:

• state your thesis
• produce evidence to support your thesis

• clearly organise your argument
• write an appropriate conclusion.

Exercise 2 ▷ *Read the following task. What do you have to write about? Underline the words which help you decide.*

> *University lecturers are now able to put their lectures on the Internet for students to read and so the importance of attending face to face lectures has been reduced.*
>
> *Do you believe the use of the Internet in formal education is a good idea? What future effects will the Internet have on academic study?*

Think about the task.
1 What are your personal views on the subject?
2 What is a possible future effect?
3 Think of two pieces of evidence to support your idea.
4 Think of a personal example to support your idea.

Exercise 3 ▷ **a** *Read a sample answer by a student. What is his view? Do you agree?*

> Over the past few years, computer technology has started to change many aspects of our lives. One of these is our approach to teaching and learning. Many people believe that the Internet will greatly enhance students' lives but in my opinion, the costs will outweigh the benefits.
>
> One future effect of the Internet on academic study is that the level of lecturer/student contact that we are used to may be reduced. This might happen simply because students do not need to spend so much time on the university campus. The same may be true of lecturers. If they are able to put their lectures on the Internet, they may choose to do this from home and so be less available for consultation. In my view this would be a great disadvantage. In my home country, tutors usually stress the importance of regular, informal meetings and students' work could suffer if efforts are not made to maintain these.
>
> Apart from the negative impact that the Internet may have on student/lecturer relationships, I think we also have to consider the disadvantages to student health. Studying is by nature a very sedentary activity involving long hours reading books and writing assignments. In addition, these activities are usually done alone. Going to campus offers students a change of scenery, a bit of exercise, and an opportunity to meet and socialise with other students. If it is no longer necessary to leave home because lectures are made available on the Internet, then students may suffer physically and mentally because of this change.
>
> Whilst I can appreciate that the internet will be a valuable source of information for students, I cannot agree that it is the best means of transmitting this information and I think we have to guard against developing an unhealthy dependence on it.

  b *Look at the sample answer again.*
1 How many paragraphs does the writer use to answer the question?
2 What is the purpose of the first and last paragraphs?
3 Now re-read each paragraph. What is the function of the first sentence in each paragraph?

Exercise 4 ▷ *An academic essay in English follows a specific conventional structure. Complete the following paragraph plan, which illustrates the structure of the sample composition:*

Exam Tip

Don't forget to include examples relevant to your experience. Remember you are not expected to be an expert on the topic. Personal experience counts!

Introduction: re-statement of topic
indication of writer's position...

Body of the composition

Paragraph 1: main ideas..
supporting ideas...

Paragraph 2: main ideas..
supporting ideas...

Conclusion: summary of views and re-statement of position...................
....

▶▶ Now go to Test 1, and try the second writing task.
Refer to the Tip Strip in Test 1 for guidelines on how to approach Task 2.

Developing writing skills 2

Organising and linking your ideas

▶ **How is your ability to organise and link your ideas assessed in IELTS?**
When writing your answer to Task 1, you will need to use appropriate linkers and structures to present the data clearly. Your answer to writing Task 2 must have a clear line of argument with relevant points that are linked well.

Exercise 5 ▷ *The writers of the sample answers to Task 1 and Task 2 (see pages 22 and 23) have used a variety of devices to link ideas. Read through the sample answers and underline all the examples of linking.*

Exercise 6 ▷ *Look at the sentences in columns A and B below and join them together using one of the linking words or phrases in the box. Use the sentences in column A first and then reverse the exercise and start with the B sentences but always keep the same overall meaning. You may need to alter or omit some of the words or use a different linking word or phrase.*

Exam Tip

When you write your answer, you must be able to demonstrate that your ideas follow a logical sequence within and across the paragraphs. If you do this, your ideas will be *coherent* or clear.

	A	B	Linking words
1	The driving test was on Friday.	I took the day off work.	and
2	The president was extremely unpopular.	The majority of people voted for the president.	so but
3	The swimming team trained hard.	The team went home unsuccessful.	because while
4	Eat your dinner.	Go to bed.	although despite the
5	I forgot to give my homework to the teacher.	My teacher didn't mark my homework.	fact that when
6	I can't comment on the film.	I haven't seen the film.	as
7	People continue to smoke.	People continue to suffer from respiratory diseases.	before since

Exercise 7 ▷ *Re-order the sentences below to create one coherent text. Underline all the words which help you to do this and say whether the link is in the meaning (i.e. lexical or in the grammatical structure i.e. grammatical).*

a Firstly money is collected at source from everyone in Australia who has a job.

b Tax on petrol is also aimed at reducing the number of vehicles on the roads by discouraging motorists from using their cars.

c The Australian government collects tax in a number of different ways.

d Income tax, as this is known, can be as high as 48% for some people.

e In addition to this tax on luxuries, there is a special tax on fuel which brings in a large amount of revenue for the government.

f Secondly, the government gains money by imposing a tax on all goods purchased or services received so that every time money changes hands a tax of 10% is paid.

g The term 'services' includes anything from getting a haircut to having your house painted.

h Another way that the government raises money is by charging an additional tax on luxuries such as wine, tobacco or perfume.

Developing writing skills 3

Writing accurately and with a good range of vocabulary

▶ **What aspects of grammar and vocabulary will be assessed by the examiner?**

There are many areas of grammar that the person marking your answer will be checking for. These include:

- verb tenses and verb agreements
- tense range
- sentence structure and word order
- spelling and punctuation.

You will also need to demonstrate that you can:

- produce a range of sentence patterns.
- use a range of vocabulary and structures.

The more mistakes you make in a piece of writing, the more difficult it is to read and make sense of what you are trying to say.

Exam Tip

It is easy to make mistakes when you are under pressure so it is vital to leave time to check your answer for mistakes before you hand in your work.

Exercise 8 ▷ **a** *Rewrite the following paragraph to improve its grammatical accuracy:*

This graph shows that how much money was spent on different products over a ten years period. Those products are computers, telephones and video cameras. The areas shown are Asia, Europe and United States. Now let describing the information shown.

b *Rewrite the following General Training Task 1 introductory paragraph to improve its grammatical accuracy. Try to improve on the style at the same time. Remember to avoid repetition and to use conjunctions to join sentences together.*

Dear Sir/Madam

I'm writing to request my bag that I left on the train when I am travelled to Dover. When I arrived home, I realised that I had left my bag in your train. Would you mind to check my bag in your lost property please! My bag is just a black small bag with the handle on a top. Inside of my bag are some of my personal possessions and my certificate from the English course that I studied in.

The IELTS Speaking Module is designed to allow you to demonstrate your oral skills in a variety of situations. These situations are similar to those you may meet at university in an English-speaking environment where you will be expected to speak in front of your colleagues in tutorials and to discuss issues relevant to your area of study, both with your lecturers and with other students.

In the course of the interview you will be expected to:

▶ answer the examiner's questions fully.

▶ speak at some length on a particular topic.

▶ express and justify your opinions on a range of topics.

| **Developing speaking skills 1** | ## Answering questions fully |

In Part 1 of the interview, the examiner will ask you questions based on everyday topics and your personal experiences.

▶ **What is a 'full answer'?**

Imagine you have been asked the following question:

> How long have you lived in this country?

Now read two possible answers to this question:

a) Eight months.

b) Eight months in total. I lived in Bristol for the first three months and then I moved to London.

Answer b) is better because it includes some additional information.

Exercise 1 ▷ *Think of answers to the following questions. In each case, try to expand your answer to include at least one piece of additional information.*

- What is the capital of your country?
- Have you got any brothers or sisters?

- What languages can you speak?
- What do you like to do in your free time?

When expanding answers, you will have to make sure that the extra information is relevant and that you have not strayed from the original topic of the question.

Exercise 2 ▷ **a** *Imagine you have been asked the following question.*

> What subject would you like to study at university?

What additional information could you give to expand your answer?

b *Now read this student's answer.*

> I'd like to study Chemical Engineering.

Exam Tip

Always try to include at least one additional piece of information. If you don't do this, your examiner will probably ask you a related follow-up question anyway.

Which of the following options are appropriate follow-up statements? Put a tick next to them. Which stray from the topic? Put a cross next to them.

1 *But first I'll have to pass several general Chemistry exams.*
2 *I am really looking forward to studying in this country.*
3 *My mother is a chemical engineer, so I've always been interested in the field.*
4 *I expect that life at university will be very different from life at school.*
5 *I'm interested in working as an industrial chemist.*
6 *I'm hoping to win a scholarship.*

Developing speaking skills 2

Long turn

▶ **What is a 'long turn'?**

In Part 2 of the interview, the examiner will ask you to speak for one to two minutes on a subject which he or she will give you on a card. This is known as a long turn.

You will have a minute to prepare and can make some notes. You should use your minute to jot down some ideas or key points to help you organise your thoughts. Do not try writing out your whole speech.

Exercise 3 ▷ *Imagine that you have been given the following topic:*

> Talk about a person from your childhood whom you particularly admired. You should mention
> * your relationship to him or her
> * what he or she did
> * what you admired about this person

a *Which of the following points would you include in your talk? Put a tick next to them:*

* the person's appearance
* their home
* reasons why you liked them
* the name of the person
* their hobbies
* your relationship to the person

Are there any other points that you would like to include?
Now think of the order in which you would discuss these points.

b Look at this student's notes made during the one-minute preparation time.

> Mr Popov — sports teacher — tall
> Olympic champ — Atlanta 1996
> Water polo
> Encouraged students — healthy lifestyle
> Good teacher — popular

Now look at this student's response to the Part 2 task based on these notes:

A person I really used to admire when I was a school student was the sports teacher - Mr Popov. I think I admired him because he was a sort of hero to us all and also because he was very tall. He'd been an Olympic athlete in the Atlanta Olympics in 1996. As far as I remember, he was in the national water polo team - though I don't think he ever actually won a medal or anything like that. But for us, just the fact that he'd been in the team, you know ... representing our country ... was enough to make him a hero. In fact, he was a good teacher and he always encouraged us to do our best in sport, even if we weren't very good at it. He used to say 'It doesn't matter if you win or not. The important thing is to do your best.' He also taught us a lot about ... health ... about staying healthy. Compared to the other teachers, he seemed to be more ... more interested in us, though perhaps it's easier to admire an Olympic champion than ... say ... a maths teacher! Anyway, we all liked Mr Popov.

c Circle the words she uses to connect her ideas or make links across the text.

d Now you try the same task.

Developing speaking skills 3

Expressing and justifying your opinions

▶ **How is your ability to express your opinions tested in IELTS?**

In Part 3 of the IELTS interview, you will be asked to express your opinion on a variety of general topics. These topics will be linked thematically to the Part 2 topic. Remember that your examiner will be assessing your English, not your opinion.

Try to make the language flow naturally and remember to keep going.

Exercise 4 ▷ **a** Look at exchanges 1–6 on page 29 ; in each case the examiner's question is in bold. In each answer, the student is giving his/her opinion on a particular subject. Circle the phrases the speaker uses to introduce his/her opinions. The first one is done for you.

b The examiner will follow a logical line of inquiry. Look at exchanges 2–6 again. What questions do you think the examiner might ask next? The first one is done for you.

1

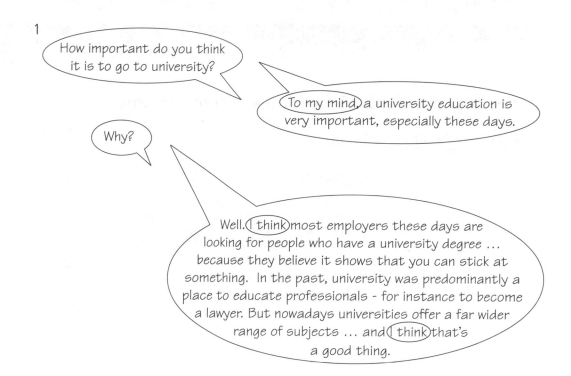

How important do you think it is to go to university?

To my mind, a university education is very important, especially these days.

Why?

Well. I think most employers these days are looking for people who have a university degree … because they believe it shows that you can stick at something. In the past, university was predominantly a place to educate professionals - for instance to become a lawyer. But nowadays universities offer a far wider range of subjects … and I think that's a good thing.

2 *How does living in a city compare with living in a small town?*
Living in a small town is, in my opinion, far less stressful than living in a crowded city.

3 *How can we encourage more people to use public transport?*
Well, I'm convinced that if buses and trains were cheaper more people would leave their cars at home.

4 *Do you believe that it should be compulsory to study a foreign language?*
No, I don't believe that being able to speak a foreign language is necessarily useful. It depends on the language, I suppose.

5 *What role do museums play in our society?*
Personally, I believe they have an important role to play. They give us a sense of history.

6 *How important is sport in the school curriculum?*
One of the best things about sport at school is that it encourages children to work together as well as helping to keep them fit.

c *Think of other phrases which can be used to give opinions and write them in the box below.*

```



```

d *Read the opinions expressed by the speakers in Exercise 4 again.*

Now work with a partner. Take turns to say how you feel about these issues. Try asking each other follow-up questions based on the answers you receive from your partner.

TEST 1

Listening module (30 minutes + transfer time)

SECTION 1   *Questions 1–10*

Tip Strip
- Note how many different **types of questions** there are. In this case, there are four: multiple choice, note completion, selecting from a list and short answer.
- Look at the instructions for each set of questions.
- Read the questions; try to predict the context of the conversation.
- Look at the questions again to see exactly what information you must listen out for.
- Underline any key words in the main part of the questions with options. Then look at the options and make sure you understand how they differ from each other.

Questions 1–3

Listen to the telephone conversation between a student and the owner of a paragliding school and answer the questions below.

Circle the correct letters A–D.

> *Example*
>
> Which course does the man suggest?
>
> **A**   2 day   **C**   5 day
>
> **(B)**   4 day   **D**   6 day

1   How much is the beginner's course?

   A $190

   B $320

   C $330

   D $430

2   What does the club insurance cover?

   A   injury to yourself

   B   injury to your equipment

   C   damage to other people's property

   D   loss of personal belongings

3   How do the girls want to travel?

   A   public transport

   B   private bus

   C   car

   D   bicycle

Questions 4–7

Complete the form below.

*Write **NO MORE THAN THREE WORDS** for each answer.*

TELEPHONE MEMO

Name: Maria Gentle

Address: C/o Mr & Mrs **4** ....

5 .... Newcastle

Fax no: 0249 **6** ....

Type of Card : **7** ....

Tip Strip

Questions 8 &9: You must get both parts of the question right to get your mark. The correct answer may not be the actual words which you hear on the tape. Option E in Question 8 is an example of this. Be on the lookout for paraphrasing of this type.

Question 8

*Circle **TWO** letters **A–G**.*

Which **TWO** of the following items must people take with them?

A sandals	**D** shirt with long sleeves	**G** sunglasses
B old clothes	**E** soft drinks	
C pullover	**F** hat	

Question 9

*Circle **TWO** letters **A–G**.*

Which **TWO** accommodation options mentioned are near the paragliding school?

A camping	**D** backpackers' inn	**G** cheap hotel
B youth hostel	**E** caravan park	
C family	**F** bed and breakfast	

Tip Strip

Question 10 is a different type of question. Make sure you are listening out for the answer.

Question 10

*Write **NO MORE THAN THREE WORDS** for your answer.*

Which weekend do the girls decide to go?

....

Questions 11–20

Complete the notes below.

Write **NO MORE THAN THREE WORDS** *for each answer.*

GOODWOOD CAR SHOW

Type of car: Duesenberg J-type

Number made: **11** ....

Type of body: **12** ....

Engines contained capsules of mercury to ensure a **13** .... trip.

Top speed: **14** .... per hour.

Sold as a **15** .... and ....

Main attraction: **16** ....

Type of car: Leyat Helica

Number built: **17** ....

Car looks like a **18** .... without **19** ....

Steering used the **20** ....

Tip Strip

- Section 2 is always a talk by one speaker. Look at the questions and the title of the task. Try to guess the context from the language and the picture.
- Note that all the questions here are note completion format. Turn the notes into questions in your head, e.g. Number made = How many were made? Do this for all the questions before you listen.
- Decide what type of information is missing (noun, number, adjective?).
- The questions follow the order of the text.
- There are two parts to this listening. This will help to orientate you.

Question15: You must get both words to get your mark.

Questions 21–30

Tip Strip

- Section 3 can have between 2 and 4 people speaking. The voices will sound quite different.
- The questions follow the order of the text.
- Note how many different types of questions there are. In this case there are four: note completion, charts and diagrams, multiple choice and completing a chart.

- Look through the questions to get an idea of the topic.
- Look carefully at the graphs. Reading the questions and underlining key words will help you make sense of the graphs. e.g. Question 24: 'relative popularity ... cinemas'. Each column in the bar chart represents how popular each cinema is in relation to the other. Look at C: Which is the most popular cinema in this graph? Which is the least popular?

Questions 21– 22

Complete the notes below.

*Write **NO MORE THAN THREE WORDS** for each answer.*

Research details:

Title of project: **21** ....

Focus of project: entertainment away from **22** ....

Questions 23–26

Circle the correct letters *A–C*.

23   Which chart shows the percentage of cinema seats provided by the different cinema houses?

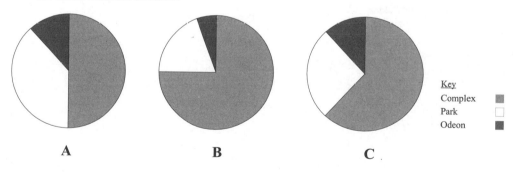

Key
Complex
Park
Odeon

A	**B**	**C**

24   Which graph shows the relative popularity of different cinemas?

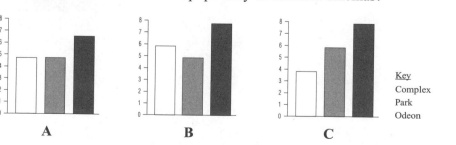

Key
Complex
Park
Odeon

A	**B**	**C**

25 What did Rosie and Mike realise about the two theatres?

    A The prices were very similar.

    B They were equally popular.

    C They offered the same facilities.

26 Which graph shows comparative attendance for cinema and theatre?

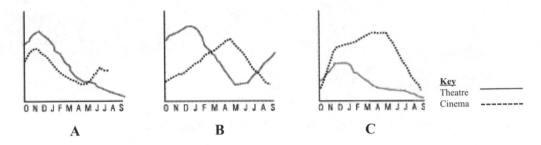

A	**B**	**C**

Questions 27–30

Complete the chart about the different music clubs below.

*Write **NO MORE THAN TWO WORDS** or use **ONE** of the symbols for each answer.*

✗ poor	✔ OK	✔✔ excellent

Tip Strip

Questions 27–30: In the middle column of the grid, you must listen for a word which means a type of music. In the right column you have to choose from three options which are already given in the box above. Make sure you use the correct symbol.

Club	Type of music	Quality of venue
The Blues Club	Blues	27 ....
The Sansue	28	✔✔
Pier Hotel	Folk	29 ....
Baldrock Café	Rock	30 ....

- Look at the questions and decide how many different types of question there are.
- Information presented in a table will have a common thread. Look at the table for Questions 33–36 and decide what information makes up this common thread. In this case there are 4 places mentioned. These place names will act as a reference for you while you listen and prevent you from getting lost.
- Note the heading at the top of the flow chart. Check that you know what kind of words are missing from the flow chart before you listen.

Questions 31 & 32 are note-completion questions. What kind of words are you looking for?

Question 32: Remember you must get both parts of the question to get your mark.

Questions 37–40: This is a flow chart. It visually represents a progression of inter-related events.

Questions 31–40

Questions 31–32

Complete the notes using **NO MORE THAN THREE WORDS** *for each answer.*

Main focus of lecture: the impact of **31** .... on the occurrence of dust storms.

Two main types of impact:

A) break up ground surface, e.g. off-road vehicle use

B) remove protective plants, e.g. **32** .... and ....…..

Questions 33–36

Complete the table using **NO MORE THAN THREE WORDS** *for each answer.*

Name of area	Details
USA 'dust bowl'	Caused by mismanagement of farmland Decade renamed the **33** ....
West Africa	Steady rise in dust storms over 20-year period
Arizona	Worst dust clouds arise from **34** .... Dust deposits are hazardous to **35** ....
Sahara	Increased wind erosion has occurred along with long-term **36** ....

Questions 37–40

Complete the flow chart using **NO MORE THAN THREE WORDS** *for each answer.*

Drying-up of Aral Sea

Intensive **37** .... in Central Asian Republics

Drop in water in major tributaries

Total volume of water in lake reduced by **38** ....

Increase in wind-blown material

Lake has become more **39** ....

Serious effects on **40** .... nearby

Reading module (1 hour)

*You should spend about 20 minutes on **Questions 1–13**, which are based on Reading Passage 1 below.*

In Praise of Amateurs

Despite the specialisation of scientific research, amateurs still have an important role to play

During the scientific revolution of the 17th century, scientists were largely men of private means who pursued their interest in natural philosophy for their own edification. Only in the past century or two has it become possible to make a living from investigating the workings of nature. Modern science was, in other words, built on the work of amateurs. Today, science is an increasingly specialised and compartmentalised subject, the domain of experts who know more and more about less and less. Perhaps surprisingly, however, amateurs – even those without private means – are still important.

A recent poll carried out at a meeting of the American Association for the Advancement of Science by astronomer Dr Richard Fienberg found that, in addition to his field of astronomy, amateurs are actively involved in such fields as acoustics, horticulture, ornithology, meteorology, hydrology and palaeontology. Far from being crackpots, amateur scientists are often in close touch with professionals, some of whom rely heavily on their co-operation.

Admittedly, some fields are more open to amateurs than others. Anything that requires expensive equipment is clearly a no-go area. And some kinds of research can be dangerous; most amateur chemists, jokes Dr Fienberg, are either locked up or have blown themselves to bits. But amateurs can make valuable contributions in fields from rocketry to palaeontology and the rise of the Internet has made it easier than ever before to collect data and distribute results.

Exactly which field of study has benefited most from the contributions of amateurs is a matter of some dispute. Dr Fienberg makes a strong case for astronomy. There is, he points out, a long tradition of collaboration between amateur and professional sky watchers. Numerous comets, asteroids and even the planet Uranus were discovered by amateurs. Today, in addition to comet and asteroid spotting, amateurs continue to do valuable work observing the brightness of variable stars and detecting novae – 'new' stars in the Milky Way and supernovae in other galaxies. Amateur observers are helpful, says Dr Fienberg, because there are so many of them (they far outnumber professionals) and because they are distributed all over the world. This makes special kinds of observations possible: if several observers around the world accurately record the time when a star is eclipsed by an asteroid, for example, it is possible to derive useful information about the asteroid's shape.

Another field in which amateurs have traditionally played an important role is palaeontology. Adrian Hunt, a palaeontologist at Mesa Technical College in New Mexico, insists that his is the field in which amateurs have made the biggest contribution. Despite the development of high-tech equipment, he says, the best sensors for finding fossils are human eyes – lots of them. Finding volunteers to look for fossils is not difficult, he says, because of the near-universal interest in anything to do with dinosaurs. As well as helping with this research, volunteers learn about science, a process he calls 'recreational education'.

Rick Bonney of the Cornell Laboratory of Ornithology in Ithaca, New York, contends that amateurs have contributed the most in his field. There are, he notes, thought to be as many as 60 million birdwatchers in America alone. Given their huge numbers and the wide geographical coverage they provide, Mr Bonney has enlisted thousands of amateurs in a number of research projects. Over the past few years their observations have uncovered previously unknown trends and cycles in bird migrations and revealed declines in the breeding populations of several species of migratory birds, prompting a habitat conservation programme.

Despite the successes and whatever the field of study, collaboration between amateurs and professionals is not without its difficulties. Not everyone, for example is happy with the term 'amateur'. Mr Bonney has coined the term 'citizen scientist' because he felt that other words, such as 'volunteer' sounded disparaging. A more serious problem is the question of how professionals can best acknowledge the contributions made by amateurs. Dr Fienberg says that some amateur astronomers are happy to provide their observations but grumble about not being reimbursed for out-of-pocket expenses. Others feel let down when their observations are used in scientific papers, but they are not listed as co-authors. Dr Hunt says some amateur palaeontologists are disappointed when told that they cannot take finds home with them.

These are legitimate concerns but none seems insurmountable. Provided amateurs and professionals agree the terms on which they will work together beforehand, there is no reason why co-operation between the two groups should not flourish. Last year Dr S. Carlson, founder of the Society for Amateur Scientists won an award worth $290,000 for his work in promoting such co-operation. He says that one of the main benefits of the prize is the endorsement it has given to the contributions of amateur scientists, which has done much to silence critics among those professionals who believe science should remain their exclusive preserve.

At the moment, says Dr Carlson, the society is involved in several schemes including an innovative rocket-design project and the setting up of a network of observers who will search for evidence of a link between low-frequency radiation and earthquakes. The amateurs, he says, provide enthusiasm and talent, while the professionals provide guidance 'so that anything they do discover will be taken seriously'. Having laid the foundations of science, amateurs will have much to contribute to its ever-expanding edifice.

Questions 1–8

Tip Strip

- Read through the summary at normal speed so that you have a fair idea of what it is about.
- Check the instructions: you can use a maximum of two words for each answer and these words must be taken from the reading passage. If you use more than two words or words that are not in the passage, the answer will be marked wrong.
- Skim the passage and find out where the part that has been summarised begins.

- Read the text around each gap carefully. See if you can predict the answer or the kind of word(s) that you are looking for.
- Select the best word from the text for each gap
- Re-read the summary, with the words you have selected for each gap, to make sure that it makes sense both grammatically and in terms of meaning.

*Complete the summary below. Choose **ONE** or **TWO WORDS** from the passage for each answer.*

Write your answers in boxes 1–8 on your answer sheet.

Summary

Prior to the 19th century, professional … **1** … did not exist and scientific research was largely carried out by amateurs. However, while … **2** … today is mostly the domain of professionals, a recent US survey highlighted the fact that amateurs play an important role in at least seven … **3** … and indeed many professionals are reliant on their … **4** … . In areas such as astronomy, amateurs can be invaluable when making specific … **5** … on a global basis. Similarly in the area of palaeontology their involvement is invaluable and helpers are easy to recruit because of the popularity of … **6** … . Amateur birdwatchers also play an active role and their work has led to the establishment of a … **7** … . Occasionally the term 'amateur' has been the source of disagreement and alternative names have been suggested but generally speaking, as long as the professional scientists … **8** … the work of the non-professionals, the two groups can work productively together.

*Reading Passage 1 contains a number of opinions provided by four different scientists. Match each opinion (Questions 9–13) with the scientists **A–D**.*

NB You may use any of the scientists A–D more than once.

9 Amateur involvement can also be an instructive pastime.

10 Amateur scientists are prone to accidents.

11 Science does not belong to professional scientists alone.

12 In certain areas of my work, people are a more valuable resource than technology.

13 It is important to give amateurs a name which reflects the value of their work.

A	Dr Fienberg
B	Adrian Hunt
C	Rick Bonney
D	Dr Carlson

READING THE SCREEN

Are the electronic media exacerbating illiteracy and making our children stupid?
On the contrary, says **Colin McCabe**, *they have the potential to make us truly literate*

The debate surrounding literacy is one of the most charged in education. On the one hand there is an army of people convinced that traditional skills of reading and writing are declining. On the other, a host of progressives protest that literacy is much more complicated than a simple technical mastery of reading and writing. This second position is supported by most of the relevant academic work over the past 20 years. These studies argue that literacy can only be understood in its social and technical context. In Renaissance England, for example, many more people could read than could write, and within reading there was a distinction between those who could read print and those who could manage the more difficult task of reading manuscript. An understanding of these earlier periods helps us understand today's 'crisis in literacy' debate.

There does seem to be evidence that there has been an overall decline in some aspects of reading and writing – you only need to compare the tabloid newspapers of today with those of 50 years ago to see a clear decrease in vocabulary and simplification of syntax. But the picture is not uniform and doesn't readily demonstrate the simple distinction between literate and illiterate which had been considered adequate since the middle of the 19th century.

While reading a certain amount of writing is as crucial as it has ever been in industrial societies, it is doubtful whether a fully extended grasp of either is as necessary as it was 30 or 40 years ago. While print retains much of its authority as a source of topical information, television has increasingly usurped this role. The ability to write fluent letters has been undermined by the telephone and research suggests that for many people the only use for writing, outside formal education, is the compilation of shopping lists.

The decision of some car manufacturers to issue their instructions to mechanics as a video pack rather than as a handbook might be taken to spell the end of any automatic link between industrialisation and literacy. On the other hand, it is also the case that ever-increasing numbers of people make their living out of writing, which is better rewarded than ever before. Schools are generally seen as institutions where the book rules – film, television and recorded sound have almost no place; but it is not clear that this opposition is appropriate. While you may not need to read and write to watch television, you certainly need to be able to read and write in order to make programmes.

Those who work in the new media are anything but illiterate. The traditional oppositions between old and new media are inadequate for understanding the world which a young child now encounters. The computer has re-established a central place for the written word on the screen, which used to be entirely devoted to the image. There is even anecdotal evidence that children are mastering reading and writing in order to get on to the Internet. There is no reason why the new and old media cannot be integrated in schools to provide the skills to become economically productive and politically enfranchised.

Nevertheless, there is a crisis in literacy and it would be foolish to ignore it. To understand that literacy may be declining because it is less central to some aspects of everyday life is not the same as acquiescing in this state of affairs. The production of school work with the new technologies could be a significant stimulus to literacy. How should these new technologies be introduced into the schools? It isn't enough to call for computers, camcorders and edit suites in every classroom; unless they are properly integrated into the educational culture, they will stand unused. Evidence suggests that this is the fate of most information technology used in the classroom. Similarly, although media studies are now part of the national curriculum, and more and more students are now clamouring to take these course, teachers remain uncertain about both methods and aims in this area.

This is not the fault of the teachers. The entertainment and information industries must be drawn into a debate with the educational institutions to determine how best to blend these new technologies into the classroom.

Many people in our era are drawn to the pessimistic view that the new media are destroying old skills and eroding critical judgement. It may be true that past generations were more literate but – taking the pre-19th century meaning of the term – this was true of only a small section of the population. The word literacy is a 19th-century coinage to describe the divorce of reading and writing from a full knowledge of literature. The education reforms of the 19th century produced reading and writing as skills separable from full participation in the cultural heritage.

The new media now point not only to a futuristic cyber-economy, they also make our cultural past available to the whole nation. Most children's access to these treasures is initially through television. It is doubtful whether our literary heritage has ever been available to or sought out by more than about 5 per cent of the population; it has certainly not been available to more than 10 per cent. But the new media joined to the old, through the public service tradition of British broadcasting, now makes our literary tradition available to all.

Tip Strip

- The questions follow the order of information in the passage.
- Read the first question and the four options A–D. One of these completes the statement so that it expresses an idea that is also given in the passage.
- Decide whether the question focuses on a detail in the passage or a main idea.
- Note the key words in the question. These will help you locate the area of the passage where you will find the answer.
- Read this part of the passage very carefully. You will find that some of the vocabulary in options A–D also occurs in the passage but only one of the options will complete the sentence correctly.

Questions 14–17

Choose the appropriate letters A–D and write them in boxes 14–17 on your answer sheet.

14 When discussing the debate on literacy in education, the writer notes that

    A children cannot read and write as well as they used to.

    B academic work has improved over the last 20 years.

    C there is evidence that literacy is related to external factors.

    D there are opposing arguments that are equally convincing.

15 In the 4th paragraph, the writer's main point is that

    A the printed word is both gaining and losing power.

    B all inventions bring disadvantages as well as benefits.

    C those who work in manual jobs no longer need to read.

    D the media offers the best careers for those who like writing.

16 According to the writer, the main problem that schools face today is

    A how best to teach the skills of reading and writing.

    B how best to incorporate technology into classroom teaching.

    C finding the means to purchase technological equipment.

    D managing the widely differing levels of literacy amongst pupils.

17 At the end of the article, the writer is suggesting that

    A literature and culture cannot be divorced.

    B the term 'literacy' has not been very useful.

    C 10 per cent of the population never read literature.

    D our exposure to cultural information is likely to increase.

Questions 18–23

Tip Strip

Questions 18–23 test your understanding of what the writer believes; i.e. his/her views or opinions. There are three choices: **Yes** – the writer believes this; **No** – the writer believes the opposite of this; **Not Given** – the writer doesn't give any views on this.

- The questions follow the order of information in the passage.
- Start with the first question and note the key words.
- Skim or scan the passage until you come to the part where the writer is discussing his/her views on the topic or idea presented in the question. If you cannot find any information on this, the answer may be 'not given'. Check this carefully.
- If you do find some information, decide whether the writer's views are the same or the opposite of those given in the question.

Do the following statements agree with the views of the writer in Reading Passage 2?

In boxes 18–23 on your answer sheet write

YES   *if the statement agrees with the writer*
NO   *if the statement contradicts the writer*
NOT GIVEN *if it is impossible to say what the writer thinks about this*

18 It is not as easy to analyse literacy levels as it used to be.

19 Our literacy skills need to be as highly developed as they were in the past.

20 Illiteracy is on the increase.

21 Professional writers earn relatively more than they used to.

22 A good literacy level is important for those who work in television.

23 Computers are having a negative impact on literacy in schools.

Questions 24–26

Complete the sentences below with words taken from Reading Passage 2.

*Write your answers in boxes 24–26 on your answer sheet. Use **NO MORE THAN THREE WORDS** for each answer.*

In Renaissance England, the best readers were those able to read … **24** … .

The writer uses the example of … **25** …to illustrate the general fall in certain areas of literacy.

It has been shown that after leaving school, the only things that a lot of people write are … **26** … .

Tip Strip
- The questions follow the order of information in the passage.
- Check the instructions: you can use a maximum of three words for each answer and these words must be taken from the reading passage. If you use more than three words or words that are not in the passage, the answer will be marked wrong.
- Read the sentences and underline the key words.
- Read the words around each gap carefully. See if you can predict the answer or the kind of word(s) that you are looking for.
- Scan or skim the passage until you come to the part that is relevant.
- Re-read the sentence with the word you have chosen for the gap to check that it makes sense both grammatically and in terms of meaning.

You should spend about 20 minutes on **Questions 27–40,** which are based on Reading Passage 3 below.

Questions 27–33

*Reading Passage 3 has seven paragraphs **A–G**.*

*From the list of headings below choose the most suitable heading for each paragraph. Write the appropriate numbers (**i–x**) in boxes 27–33 on your answer sheet.*

Tip Strip

• Although the instructions ask you to choose the 'most suitable' heading, each heading will only fit one paragraph.

• Read through the list of headings. Note that each heading expresses a main idea.

• There are ten headings and seven questions, so three of the headings do not fit any of the paragraphs.

• Skim through the whole passage so that you have a good idea of what it is about.

• Read each paragraph carefully, noting the main idea or theme. Do not worry if there are words that you do not understand.

• Select the heading that best describes the main idea of the paragraph.

List of headings

i	The long-term impact
ii	A celebrated achievement
iii	Early brilliance passes unrecognised
iv	Outdated methods retain popularity
v	The basis of a new design is born
vi	Frustration at never getting the design right
vii	Further refinements meet persistent objections
viii	Different in all respects
ix	Bridge-makers look elsewhere
x	Transport developments spark a major change

---

27   Paragraph A

28   Paragraph B

29   Paragraph C

30   Paragraph D

31   Paragraph E

32   Paragraph F

33   Paragraph G

The Revolutionary Bridges of Robert Maillart

Swiss engineer Robert Maillart built some of the greatest bridges of the 20th century. His designs elegantly solved a basic engineering problem: how to support enormous weights using a slender arch

A   Just as railway bridges were the great structural symbols of the 19th century, highway bridges became the engineering emblems of the 20th century. The invention of the automobile created an irresistible demand for paved roads and vehicular bridges throughout the developed world. The type of bridge needed for cars and trucks, however, is fundamentally different from that needed for locomotives. Most highway bridges carry lighter loads than railway bridges do, and their roadways can be sharply curved or steeply sloping. To meet these needs, many turn-of-the-century bridge designers began working with a new building material: reinforced concrete, which has steel bars embedded in it. And the master of this new material was Swiss structural engineer, Robert Maillart.

B   Early in his career, Maillart developed a unique method for designing bridges, buildings and other concrete structures. He rejected the complex mathematical analysis of loads and stresses that was being enthusiastically adopted by most of his contemporaries. At the same time, he also eschewed the decorative approach taken by many bridge builders of his time. He resisted imitating architectural styles and adding design elements solely for ornamentation. Maillart's method was a form of creative intuition. He had a knack for conceiving new shapes to solve classic engineering problems. And because he worked in a highly competitive field, one of his goals was economy – he won design and construction contracts because his structures were reasonably priced, often less costly than all his rivals' proposals.

C   Maillart's first important bridge was built in the small Swiss town of Zuoz. The local officials had initially wanted a steel bridge to span the 30-metre wide Inn River, but Maillart argued that he could build a more elegant bridge made of reinforced concrete for about the same cost. His crucial innovation was incorporating the bridge's arch and roadway into a form called the hollow-box arch, which would substantially reduce the bridge's expense by minimising the amount of concrete needed. In a conventional arch bridge the weight of the roadway is transferred by columns to the arch, which must be relatively thick. In Maillart's design, though, the roadway and arch were connected by three vertical walls, forming two hollow boxes running under the roadway (*see diagram*). The big advantage of this design was that because the arch would not have to bear the load alone, it could be much thinner – as little as one-third as thick as the arch in the conventional bridge.

D His first masterpiece, however, was the 1905 Tavanasa Bridge over the Rhine river in the Swiss Alps. In this design, Maillart removed the parts of the vertical walls which were not essential because they carried no load. This produced a slender, lighter-looking form, which perfectly met the bridge's structural requirements. But the Tavanasa Bridge gained little favourable publicity in Switzerland; on the contrary, it aroused strong aesthetic objections from public officials who were more comfortable with old-fashioned stone-faced bridges. Maillart, who had founded his own construction firm in 1902, was unable to win any more bridge projects, so he shifted his focus to designing buildings, water tanks and other structures made of reinforced concrete and did not resume his work on concrete bridges until the early 1920s.

E His most important breakthrough during this period was the development of the deck-stiffened arch, the first example of which was the Flienglibach Bridge, built in 1923. An arch bridge is somewhat like an inverted cable. A cable curves downward when a weight is hung from it, an arch bridge curves upward to support the roadway and the compression in the arch balances the dead load of the traffic. For aesthetic reasons, Maillart wanted a thinner arch and his solution was to connect the arch to the roadway with transverse walls. In this way, Maillart justified making the arch as thin as he could reasonably build it. His analysis accurately predicted the behaviour of the bridge but the leading authorities of Swiss engineering would argue against his methods for the next quarter of a century.

F Over the next 10 years, Maillart concentrated on refining the visual appearance of the deck-stiffened arch. His best-known structure is the Salginatobel Bridge, completed in 1930. He won the competition for the contract because his design was the least expensive of the 19 submitted – the bridge and road were built for only 700,000 Swiss francs, equivalent to some $3.5 million today. Salginatobel was also Maillart's longest span, at 90 metres and it had the most dramatic setting of all his structures, vaulting 80 metres above the ravine of the Salgina brook. In 1991 it became the first concrete bridge to be designated an international historic landmark.

G Before his death in 1940, Maillart completed other remarkable bridges and continued to refine his designs. However, architects often recognised the high quality of Maillart's structures before his fellow engineers did and in 1947 the architectural section of the Museum of Modern Art in New York City devoted a major exhibition entirely to his works. In contrast, very few American structural engineers at that time had even heard of Maillart. In the following years, however, engineers realised that Maillart's bridges were more than just aesthetically pleasing – they were technically unsurpassed. Maillart's hollow-box arch became the dominant design form for medium and long-span concrete bridges in the US. In Switzerland, professors finally began to teach Maillart's ideas, which then influenced a new generation of designers.

Tip Strip

- Check the instructions for **Questions 34–36**: you can use a maximum of two words for each answer and these words must be taken from the reading passage. If you use more than two words or words that are not in the passage, the answer will be marked wrong.
- Skim/scan the passage until you come to the section that describes the two types of bridge.
- Read this part very carefully and select the words in the passage that fit the labels.

Questions 34–36

*Complete the labels on the diagrams below using **ONE** or **TWO WORDS** from the reading passage. Write your answers in boxes 34–36 on your answer sheet.*

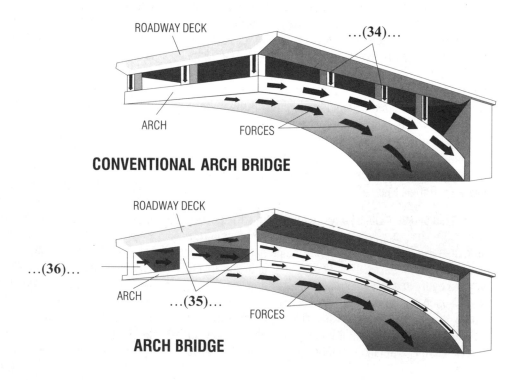

CONVENTIONAL ARCH BRIDGE

ARCH BRIDGE

Tip Strip

- The part-statements or questions follow the order of information in the passage.
- There are four part-statements and seven endings so some of the endings will not be used at all.
- Many of the endings A–G will fit each question grammatically.
- You have already read the passage at least once. Can you guess any of the answers?
- Do not re-read the whole passage. Underline the keywords in each statement, then scan the passage for these words, e.g. Question 37: <u>the hollow-box arch</u>.
- When you find the relevant part of the passage, read it very carefully. Question 37: Which paragraph discusses the design of hollow-box arch?
- Select the option that best completes each sentence.
- Re-read the completed sentence and compare this for meaning with the appropriate section of the passage.

Questions 37–40

Complete each of the following statements (Questions 37–40) with the best ending (A–G) from the box below.

Write the appropriate letters A–G in boxes 37–40 on your answer sheet.

37 Maillart designed the hollow-box arch in order to ......

38 Following the construction of the Tavanasa Bridge, Maillart failed to ......

39 The transverse walls of the Flienglibach Bridge allowed Maillart to ......

40 Of all his bridges, the Salginatobel enabled Maillart to ......

A ...... prove that local people were wrong.

B ...... find work in Switzerland.

C ...... win more building commissions.

D ...... reduce the amount of raw material required.

E ...... recognise his technical skills.

F ...... capitalise on the spectacular terrain.

G ...... improve the appearance of his bridges.

Writing module (1 hour)

You should spend about 20 minutes on this task.

The graph below shows how money was spent on different forms of entertainment over a five-year period.

Write a report for a university lecturer describing the information shown below.

You should write at least 150 words.

Tip Strip

- Read the question very carefully.
- The instructions state that you should 'describe' the information in the graph. You should NOT speculate about the reasons for the data or give reasons for it.
- Look carefully at the labels. What do the diagrams represent?
- Take a minute to plan how you will describe the information. Are there any significant features? Can you compare or contrast any of the data?
- Think of how best to group the information in the diagram.
- Write one or two paragraphs, making sure that you cover all the important points.
- Read through your answer when you have finished and check grammar, spelling and punctuation.
- Check that you have linked your points together well.
- Make sure you have written enough words. You will not be penalised for writing too much but keep an eye on the time: you will need to leave about 40 minutes for Task 2.

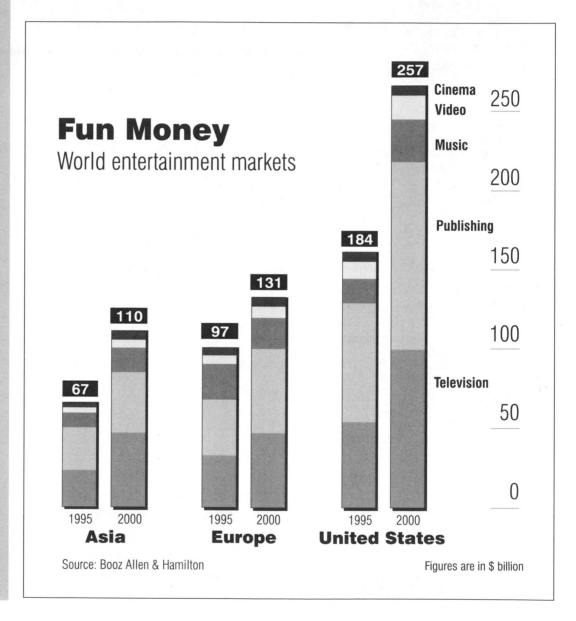

Fun Money
World entertainment markets

Cinema
Video
Music
Publishing
Television

257
184
131
110
97
67

1995 2000 1995 2000 1995 2000
Asia **Europe** **United States**

250
200
150
100
50
0

Source: Booz Allen & Hamilton

Figures are in $ billion

You should spend about 40 minutes on this task.

Present a written argument or case to an educated non-specialist audience on the following topic:

> *Under British and Australian laws a jury in a criminal case has no access to information about the defendant's past criminal record. This protects the person who is being accused of the crime.*
>
> *Some lawyers have suggested that this practice should be changed and that a jury should be given all the past facts before they reach their decision about the case.*
>
> *Do you agree or disagree? Give reasons for your answer.*

You should write at least 250 words.

You should use your own ideas, knowledge and experience and support your arguments with examples and relevant evidence.

Speaking module (11–14 minutes)

PART 1

Tip Strip

- The examiners want you to perform to the best of your ability and the test is designed to give you every opportunity to speak, but examiners can only rate what they hear from you. So make sure you speak up and use the time as effectively as possible.

- In **Part 1**, if the examiner asks you a question which can be answered by 'Yes' or 'No', try to give some extra information to extend your answer. Yes/No questions in English are often an invitation to say more.

- Make sure you answer the question you are asked. Do not come to the interview with a learned talk.

The examiner will ask you questions about yourself, such as:

- ¥ *What's your name?*
- ¥ *Where do you live?*
- ¥ *What family members do you live with?*
- ¥ *What are you studying?*
- ¥ *What do you like about your studies?*
- ¥ *What do you like about learning English?*
- ¥ *How often do you use English?*

PART 2

Tip Strip

- In **Part 2**, try to make your talk as interesting as possible. You have a minute to prepare what you are going to say and you can make some notes. Write down some key words or ideas only. Do not write out everything you are going to say.

- Look carefully at the prompt card on this page. Think of a city which impressed you.

- Think of 2 or 3 things you really remember about the city. Try to interest the examiner in what you say.

The topic for your talk will be written on a card which the examiner will hand you. Read it carefully and then make some brief notes.

A city you have visited

INSTRUCTIONS
Please read the topic below carefully. You will be asked to talk about it for 1 to 2 minutes.
You have one minute to think about what you re going to say.
You can make some notes to help you if you wish.

Describe a city you have visited which has impressed you.

You should say: where it is situated

why you visited it

what you liked about it

At the end of your talk, the examiner will ask one or two brief questions to signal that it is time to stop talking. For example, he or she might ask you:

Do you like cities generally?
Would you like to live in the city you spoke about?

Once your talk in Part 2 is over, your examiner will ask you further questions related to the topic in Part 2. The examiner may ask you to speak about these points.

Tip Strip

- Look at the follow-up discussion ideas for Part 3 on this page. See how they are broadly linked to the topic of Part 2.
- Make a few notes in response to each of the prompts given here. The discussion could take any of these directions.
- Try to think of at least five other interesting ideas linked to this topic. Remember! You can take the discussion in a direction of your choice, if it is appropriately linked.
- Don't be afraid to take the initiative in Part 3 of the speaking test. This is your chance to show your fluency, your ability to give and support an opinion and your range of grammatical forms and vocabulary.

A city you have visited

- *advantages of living in a big city*

- *negative aspects of crowded cities*

- *architectural design*

- *paying for the services*

- *transport*

TEST 2

Listening module (30 minutes + transfer time)

Questions 1–10

Questions 1–4

Circle the correct letters A–C.

> *Example*
>
> Which course is the man interested in?
>
> **A**   English
>
> **B**   Mandarin
>
> Ⓒ   Japanese

Tip Strip

- Look at the questions and decide how many different types of question there are.

- Read the multiple-choice options and underline any important words. Note! There is always an example of the first question type in Section 1.

1   What kind of course is the man seeking?

    A   Daytime

    B   Evenings

    C   Weekends

2   How long does the man want to study?

    A   12 weeks

    B   6 months

    C   8 months

3   What proficiency level is the student?

    A   Beginner

    B   Intermediate

    C   Advanced

4   When does the man want to start the course?

    A   March

    B   June

    C   September

Questions 5–10

Complete the form.
*Write **NO MORE THAN THREE WORDS** for each answer.*

Tip Strip

• Look at the form. Decide what kind of information you will need to write. There is often a name or an address in this type of question. You must spell the name correctly, as it is given on the tape.

Language Centre
Client Information Card

Name: Richard **5** ....

E-mail address: **6** ....@hotmail.com

Date of birth: **7** 1980

Reason for studying Japanese: **8**...

Specific learning needs: **9** ....

Place of previous study (if any): **10**..

Questions 11–20

Questions 11–12

Complete the sentences below.

*Write **NO MORE THAN THREE WORDS** for each answer.*

11 The story illustrates that dogs are ………………….. animals.

12 The people of the town built a ………………….. of a dog.

Questions 13–20

Complete the table below.
*Write **NO MORE THAN THREE WORDS** for each answer.*

TYPE OF WORKING DOG	ESSENTIAL CHARACTERISTICS FOR THE JOB	ADDITIONAL INFORMATION
Sheep dogs	Smart, obedient	Herd sheep and **13** …………….. them
Guide dogs	Confident and **14** ………………..	Training paid for by **15** ………………….
Guard dogs and **16** …………….. and …………….. dogs	Tough and courageous	Dogs and trainers available through **17** ………………….
Detector dogs	Need to really **18** ……………….	In Sydney they catch **19** …………….. a month
Transport dogs	Happy working **20** ………………..	International treaty bans huskies from Antarctica

Questions 21–30

Questions 21–23

Complete the notes below.

Write NO MORE THAN THREE WORDS or A NUMBER for each answer.

Braille – a system of writing for the blind

- Louis Braille was blinded as a child in his **21** ....

- Braille invented the writing system in the year **22** ....

- An early writing system for the blind used embossed letters.

- A military system using dots was called **23** ....

Questions 24–27

Circle the correct letters A–C.

24 Which diagram shows the Braille positions?

A   B   C

25 What can the combined dots represent?

   A both letters and words

   B only individual words

   C only letters of the alphabet

26 When was the Braille system officially adopted?

   A as soon as it was invented

   B two years after it was invented

   C after Louis Braille had died

27 What is unusual about the way Braille is written?

   A It can only be written using a machine.

   B The texts have to be read backwards.

   C Handwritten Braille is created in reverse.

Questions 28–30

List THREE subjects that also use a Braille code.

Write NO MORE THAN ONE WORD for each answer.

28 ....

29 ....

30 ....

Questions 31–40

Questions 31–35

Complete the notes below.

*Write **NO MORE THAN THREE WORDS** or **A NUMBER** for each answer.*

Question: Can babies remember any **31** .... ?

Experiment with babies:

Apparatus: baby in cot

colourful mobile

some **32** ....

Re-introduce mobile between one and **33** .... later.

Table showing memory test results

Baby's age	Maximum memory span
2 months	2 days
3 months	**34** ....
21 months	several weeks
2 years	**35** ....

Questions 36–40

Research questions: Is memory linked to **36** .... development?

Can babies **37** .... their memories?

Experiment with older children:

Stages in incident: a)   lecture taking place

b)   object falls over

c)   **38** ....

Table showing memory test results

Age	% remembered next day	% remembered after 5 months
Adults	70%	**39** ....
9-year-olds	70%	Less than 60%
6-year-olds	Just under 70%	**40** ....

Reading module (1 hour)

You should spend about 20 minutes on **Questions 1–13** *which are based on Reading Passage 1 below.*

Questions 1–8

Reading Passage 1 has seven paragraphs A–H.

From the list of headings below choose the most suitable heading for each paragraph. Write the appropriate numbers (i–xi) in boxes 1–8 on your answer sheet.

List of headings

i	Obesity in animals
ii	Hidden dangers
iii	Proof of the truth
iv	New perspective on the horizon
v	No known treatment
vi	Rodent research leads the way
vii	Expert explains energy requirements of obese people
viii	A very uncommon complaint
ix	Nature or nurture
x	Shifting the blame
xi	Lifestyle change required despite new findings

---

1 Paragraph A

2 Paragraph B

3 Paragraph C

4 Paragraph D

5 Paragraph E

6 Paragraph F

7 Paragraph G

8 Paragraph H

Tackling Obesity in the Western World

A Obesity is a huge problem in many Western countries and one which now attracts considerable medical interest as researchers take up the challenge to find a 'cure' for the common condition of being seriously overweight. However, rather than take responsibility for their weight, obese people have often sought solace in the excuse that they have a slow metabolism, a genetic hiccup which sentences more than half the Australian population (63% of men and 47% of women) to a life of battling with their weight. The argument goes like this: it doesn't matter how little they eat, they gain weight because their bodies break down food and turn it into energy more slowly than those with a so-called normal metabolic rate.

B 'This is nonsense,' says Dr Susan Jebb from the Dunn Nutrition Unit at Cambridge in England. Despite the persistence of this metabolism myth, science has known for several years that the exact opposite is in fact true. Fat people have faster metabolisms than thin people. 'What is very clear,' says Dr Jebb, 'is that overweight people actually burn off more energy. They have more cells, bigger hearts, bigger lungs and they all need more energy just to keep going.'

C It took only one night, spent in a sealed room at the Dunn Unit to disabuse one of their patients of the beliefs of a lifetime: her metabolism was fast, not slow. By sealing the room and measuring the exact amount of oxygen she used, researchers were able to show her that her metabolism was not the culprit. It wasn't the answer she expected and probably not the one she wanted but she took the news philosophically.

D Although the metabolism myth has been completely disproved, science has far from discounted our genes as responsible for making us whatever weight we are, fat or thin. One of the world's leading obesity researchers, geneticist Professor Stephen O'Rahilly, goes so far as to say we are on the threshold of a complete change in the way we view not only morbid obesity, but also everyday overweight. Prof. O'Rahilly's groundbreaking work in Cambridge has proven that obesity can be caused by our genes. 'These people are not weak-willed, slothful or lazy,' says Prof. O'Rahilly, 'They have a medical condition due to a genetic defect and that causes them to be obese.'

E In Australia, the University of Sydney's Professor Ian Caterson says while major genetic defects may be rare, many people probably have minor genetic variations that combine to dictate weight and are responsible for things such as how much we eat, the amount of exercise we do and the amount of energy we need. When you add up all these little variations, the result is that some people are genetically predisposed to putting on weight. He says while the fast/slow metabolism debate may have been settled, that doesn't mean some other subtle change in the metabolism gene won't be found in overweight people. He is confident that science will, eventually, be able to 'cure' some forms of obesity but the only effective way for the vast majority of overweight and obese people to lose weight is a change of diet and an increase in exercise.

F Despite the $500 million a year Australians spend trying to lose weight and the $830 million it costs the community in health care, obesity is at epidemic proportions here, as it is in all Western nations. Until recently, research and treatment for obesity had concentrated on behaviour modification, drugs to decrease appetite and surgery. How the drugs worked was often not understood and many caused severe side effects and even death in some patients. Surgery for obesity has also claimed many lives.

G It has long been known that a part of the brain called the hypothalamus is responsible for regulating hunger, among other things. But it wasn't until 1994 that Professor Jeffery Friedman from Rockerfeller University in the US sent science in a new direction by studying an obese mouse. Prof. Friedman found that unlike its thin brothers, the fat mouse did not produce a hitherto unknown hormone called leptin. Manufactured by the fat cells, leptin acts as a messenger, sending signals to the hypothalamus to turn off the appetite. Previously, the fat cells were thought to be responsible simply for storing fat. Prof. Friedman gave the fat mouse leptin and it lost 30% of its body weight in two weeks.

H On the other side of the Atlantic, Prof. O'Rahilly read about this research with great excitement. For many months two blood samples had lain in the bottom of his freezer, taken from two extremely obese young cousins. He hired a doctor to develop a test for leptin in human blood, which eventually resulted in the discovery that neither of the children's blood contained the hormone. When one cousin was given leptin, she lost a stone in weight and Prof. O'Rahilly made medical history. Here was the first proof that a genetic defect could cause obesity in humans. But leptin deficiency turned out to be an extremely rare condition and there is a lot more research to be done before the 'magic' cure for obesity is ever found.

Questions 9–13

Complete the summary of Reading Passage 1 (Questions 9–13) using words from the box at the bottom of the page.

Write your answers in boxes 9–13 on your answer sheet.

OBESITY

Example   weight

People with a … **(0)** … problem often try to deny responsibility.

They do this by seeking to blame their … **(9)** … for the fact that they are

overweight and erroneously believe that they use … **(10)** … energy than

thin people to stay alive. However, recent research has shown that a

… **(11)** … problem can be responsible for obesity as some people seem

programmed to … **(12)** … more than others. The new research points to a shift

from trying to change people's … **(13)** … to seeking an answer to the problem

in the laboratory.

List of words

weight	exercise	sleep
mind	bodies	exercise
metabolism	more	genetic
less	physical	consume
behaviour	use	mental

Wheel of Fortune

Emma Duncan discusses the potential effects on the entertainment industry of the digital revolution

A Since moving pictures were invented a century ago, a new way of distributing entertainment to consumers has emerged about once every generation. Each such innovation has changed the industry irreversibly; each has been accompanied by a period of fear mixed with exhilaration. The arrival of digital technology, which translates music, pictures and text into the zeros and ones of computer language, marks one of those periods.

B This may sound familiar, because the digital revolution, and the explosion of choice that would go with it, has been heralded for some time. In 1992, John Malone, chief executive of TCI, an American cable giant, welcomed the '500-channel universe'. Digital television was about to deliver everything except pizzas to people's living rooms. When the entertainment companies tried out the technology, it worked fine – but not at a price that people were prepared to pay.

C Those 500 channels eventually arrived but via the Internet and the PC rather than through television. The digital revolution was starting to affect the entertainment business in unexpected ways. Eventually it will change every aspect of it, from the way cartoons are made to the way films are screened to the way people buy music. That much is clear. What nobody is sure of is how it will affect the economics of the business.

D New technologies always contain within them both threats and opportunities. They have the potential both to make the companies in the business a great deal richer, and to sweep them away. Old companies always fear new technology. Hollywood was hostile to television, television terrified by the VCR. Go back far enough, points out Hal Varian, an economist at the University of California at Berkeley, and you find publishers complaining that 'circulating libraries' would cannibalise their sales. Yet whenever a new technology has come in, it has made more money for existing entertainment companies. The proliferation of the means of distribution results, gratifyingly, in the proliferation of dollars, pounds, pesetas and the rest to pay for it.

E All the same, there is something in the old companies' fears. New technologies may not threaten their lives, but they usually change their role. Once television became widespread, film and radio stopped being the staple form of entertainment. Cable television has undermined the power of the broadcasters. And as power has shifted the movie studios, the radio companies and the television broadcasters have been swallowed up. These days, the grand old names of entertainment have more resonance than power. Paramount is part of Viacom, a cable company; Universal, part of Seagram, a drinks-and-entertainment company; MGM, once the roaring lion of Hollywood, has been reduced to a whisper because it is not part of one of the giants. And RCA, once the most important broadcasting company in the world, is now a recording label belonging to Bertelsmann, a large German entertainment company.

F Part of the reason why incumbents got pushed aside was that they did not see what was coming. But they also faced a tighter regulatory environment than the present one. In America, laws preventing television broadcasters from owning programme companies were repealed earlier this decade, allowing the creation of vertically integrated businesses. Greater freedom, combined with a sense of history, prompted the smarter companies in the entertainment business to re-invent themselves. They saw what happened to those of their predecessors who were stuck with one form of distribution. So, these days, the powers in the entertainment business are no longer movie studios, or television broadcasters, or publishers; all those businesses have become part of bigger businesses still, companies that can both create content and distribute it in a range of different ways.

G Out of all this, seven huge entertainment companies have emerged – Time Warner, Walt Disney, Bertelsmann, Viacom, News Corp, Seagram and Sony. They cover pretty well every bit of the entertainment business except pornography. Three are American, one is Australian, one Canadian, one German and one Japanese. 'What you are seeing', says Christopher Dixon, managing director of media research at PaineWebber, a stockbroker, 'is the creation of a global oligopoly. It happened to the oil and automotive businesses earlier this century; now it is happening to the entertainment business.' It remains to be seen whether the latest technology will weaken those great companies, or make them stronger than ever.

Tip Strip

- Read the rubric carefully. Each question here is a paraphrase of detailed information within paragraphs. You will need to match the information in each question to the correct paragraph.
- The questions do **not** follow the order of information in the passage.
- Read the passage once through quickly, noting any key words or main ideas within the paragraphs.
- Read through the questions and underline the key words, e.g. Question 14: 'the contrasting effects that new ...' You may be able to do some of the questions from your first reading of the passage.
- Now begin with the first question. Skim the passage for an equivalent idea, using your understanding of the themes in each paragraph to help you read more quickly. **Question 14:** Which paragraph describes the potential effects of new technology?
- You may want to select the questions that have key words that are easy to scan for and do these first, leaving the more difficult questions to later.

Questions 14–21

Reading Passage 2 has seven paragraphs A–G.

Which paragraph mentions the following (Questions 14–21)?

Write the appropriate letters (A–G) in boxes 14–21 on your answer sheet.

NB Some of the paragraphs will be used more than once.

14 the contrasting effects that new technology can have on existing business

15 the fact that a total transformation is going to take place in the future in the delivery of all forms of entertainment

16 the confused feelings that people are known to have experienced in response to technological innovation

17 the fact that some companies have learnt from the mistakes of others

18 the high cost to the consumer of new ways of distributing entertainment

19 uncertainty regarding the financial impact of wider media access

20 the fact that some companies were the victims of strict government policy

21 the fact that the digital revolution could undermine the giant entertainment companies

Questions 22–25

The writer refers to various individuals and companies in the reading passage. Match the people or companies (A–E) with the points made in Questions 22–25 about the introduction of new technology.

Write the appropriate letter (A–E) in boxes 22–25 on your answer sheet.

22 Historically, new forms of distributing entertainment have alarmed those well-established in the business.

23 The merger of entertainment companies follows a pattern evident in other industries.

24 Major entertainment bodies that have remained independent have lost their influence.

25 News of the most recent technological development was published some years ago.

A	John Malone
B	Hal Valarian
C	MGM
D	Walt Disney
E	Christopher Dixon

Questions 26–27

Choose the appropriate letters A–D and write them in boxes 26–27 on your answer sheet.

26 How does the writer put across his views on the digital revolution?

A by examining the forms of media that will be affected by it

B by analysing the way entertainment companies have reacted to it

C by giving a personal definition of technological innovation

D by drawing comparisons with other periods of technological innovation

27 Which of the following best summarises the writer's views in Reading Passage 2?

A The public should cease resisting the introduction of new technology.

B Digital technology will increase profits in the entertainment business.

C Entertainment companies should adapt to technological innovation.

D Technological change only benefits big entertainment companies.

What do we mean by being 'talented' or 'gifted'? The most obvious way is to look at the work someone does and if they are capable of significant success, label them as talented. The purely quantitative route – 'percentage definition' – looks not at individuals, but at simple percentages, such as the top five per cent of the population, and labels them – by definition – as gifted. This definition has fallen from favour, eclipsed by the advent of IQ tests, favoured by luminaries such as Professor Hans Eysenck, where a series of written or verbal tests of general intelligence leads to a score of intelligence.

The IQ test has been eclipsed in turn. Most people studying intelligence and creativity in the new millennium now prefer a broader definition, using a multifaceted approach where talents in many areas are recognised rather than purely concentrating on academic achievement. If we are therefore assuming that talented, creative or gifted individuals may need to be assessed across a range of abilities, does this mean intelligence can run in families as a genetic or inherited tendency? Mental dysfunction – such as schizophrenia – can, so is an efficient mental capacity passed on from parent to child?

Animal experiments throw some light on this question, and on the whole area of whether it is genetics, the environment or a combination of the two that allows for intelligence and creative ability. Different strains of rats show great differences in intelligence or 'rat reasoning'. If these are brought up in normal conditions and then run through a maze to reach a food goal, the 'bright' strain make far fewer wrong turns that the 'dull' ones. But if the environment is made dull and boring the number of errors becomes equal. Return the rats to an exciting maze and the discrepancy returns as before – but is much smaller. In other words, a dull rat in a stimulating environment will almost do as well as a bright rat who is bored in a normal one. This principle applies to humans too – someone may be born with innate intelligence, but their environment probably has the final say over whether they become creative or even a genius.

Evidence now exists that most young children, if given enough opportunities and encouragement, are able to achieve significant and sustainable levels of academic or sporting prowess. Bright or creative children are often physically very active at the same time, and so may receive more parental attention as a result – almost by default – in order to ensure their safety. They may also talk earlier, and this, in turn, breeds parental interest. This can sometimes cause problems with other siblings who may feel jealous even though they themselves may be bright. Their creative talents may be undervalued and so never come to fruition. Two themes seem to run through famously creative families as a result. The first is that the parents were able to identify the talents of each child, and nurture and encourage these accordingly but in an even-handed manner. Individual differences were encouraged, and friendly sibling rivalry was not seen as a particular problem. If the father is, say, a famous actor, there is no undue pressure for his children to follow him onto the boards, but instead their chosen interests are encouraged. There need not even by any obvious talent in such a family since there always needs to be someone who sets the family career in motion, as in the case of the Sheen acting dynasty.

Martin Sheen was the seventh of ten children born to a Spanish immigrant father and an Irish mother. Despite intense parental disapproval he turned his back on entrance exams to university and borrowed cash from a local priest to start a fledgling acting career. His acting successes in films such as *Badlands* and *Apocalypse Now* made him one of the most highly-regarded actors of the 1970s. Three sons – Emilio Estevez, Ramon Estevez and Charlie Sheen – have followed him into the profession as a consequence of being inspired by his motivation and enthusiasm.

A stream seems to run through creative families. Such children are not necessarily smothered with love by their parents. They feel loved and wanted, and are secure in their home, but are often more surrounded by an atmosphere of work and where following a calling appears to be important. They may see from their parents that it takes time and dedication to be master of a craft, and so are in less of a hurry to achieve for themselves once they start to work.

The generation of creativity is complex: it is a mixture of genetics, the environment, parental teaching and luck that determines how successful or talented family members are. This last point – luck – is often not mentioned where talent is concerned but plays an undoubted part. Mozart, considered by many to be the finest composer of all time, was lucky to be living in an age that encouraged the writing of music. He was brought up surrounded by it, his father was a musician who encouraged him to the point of giving up his job to promote his child genius, and he learnt musical composition with frightening speed – the speed of a genius. Mozart himself simply wanted to create the finest music ever written but did not necessarily view himself as a genius – he could write sublime music at will, and so often preferred to lead a hedonistic lifestyle that he found more exciting than writing music to order.

Albert Einstein and Bill Gates are two more examples of people whose talents have blossomed by virtue of the times they were living in. Einstein was a solitary, somewhat slow child who had affection at home but whose phenomenal intelligence emerged without any obvious parental input. This may have been partly due to the fact that at the start of the 20th Century a lot of the Newtonian laws of physics were being questioned, leaving a fertile ground for ideas such as his to be developed. Bill Gates may have had the creative vision to develop Microsoft, but without the new computer age dawning at the same time he may never have achieved the position on the world stage he now occupies.

Tip Strip

- The arrows in this diagram help you understand that you are making notes on stages or changes over time.
- Underline the key words in the instructions e.g. <u>defining talent</u>.
- Note-completion tasks are usually based on a section of the passage.
- You will locate this section by scanning the passage for the key words. Which two paragraphs discuss the definition of talent? Read this section carefully and answer Questions 28 & 29.
- Note that you can use a maximum of two words for each answer and that these words must be taken from the reading passage. If you use more than two words or words that are not in the passage, the answer will be marked wrong.

Questions 28–29

Complete the notes, which show how the approaches to defining 'talent' have changed. Choose ONE or TWO WORDS from the passage for each answer.

Write your answers in boxes 28–29 on your answer sheet.

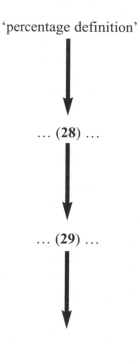

'percentage definition'

… (28) …

… (29) …

Tip Strip

- Underline the key words in the question.
- Skim through the passage until you find the relevant part or parts.
- Make sure the options that you choose are paraphrases of what is stated in the passage. Do not just match words.
- Some of the options are wrong but may be linked to ideas that are given in the passage.

Questions 30–32

Which **THREE** *of the following does the writer regard as a feature of creative families?*

Write the appropriate letters A–F in boxes 30–32 on your answer sheet.

A   a higher than average level of parental affection

B   competition between brothers and sisters

C   parents who demonstrate vocational commitment

D   strong motivation to take exams and attend university

E   a patient approach to achieving success

F   the identification of the most talented child in the family

Questions 33–34

Choose the appropriate letters A–D and write them in boxes 33–34 on your answer sheet.

33   The rat experiment was conducted to show that

    A   certain species of rat are more intelligent than others.

    B   intelligent rats are more motivated than 'dull' rats.

    C   a rat's surroundings can influence its behaviour.

    D   a boring environment has little impact on a 'bright' rat.

34   The writer cites the story of Martin Sheen to show that

    A   he was the first in a creative line.

    B   his parents did not have his creative flair.

    C   he became an actor without proper training.

    D   his sons were able to benefit from his talents.

Questions 35–39

Do the following statements agree with the claims of the writer in Reading Passage 3?

In boxes 35–39 on your answer sheet write

YES   *if the statement agrees with the writer's claims*
NO   *if the statement contradicts the writer's claims*
NOT GIVEN *if it is impossible to say what the writer thinks about this*

35   Intelligence tests have now been proved to be unreliable.

36   The brother or sister of a gifted older child may fail to fulfil their own potential.

37   The importance of luck in the genius equation tends to be ignored.

38   Mozart was acutely aware of his own remarkable talent.

39   Einstein and Gates would have achieved success in any era.

Tip Strip

Question 40 tests your global reading skills.

- Although some of the ideas in A–D may be discussed in the passage, you must decide what the WHOLE passage is about. Then choose the option that best states this.

Question 40

From the list below choose the most suitable title for the whole of Reading Passage 3.

Write the appropriate letter A–D in box 40 on your answer sheet.

A   Geniuses in their time
B   Education for the gifted
C   Revising the definition of intelligence
D   Nurturing talent within the family

Writing module (1 hour)

You should spend about 20 minutes on this task.

The graphs below show the types of music albums purchased by people in Britain according to sex and age.

Write a report for a university lecturer describing the information shown below.

You should write at least 150 words.

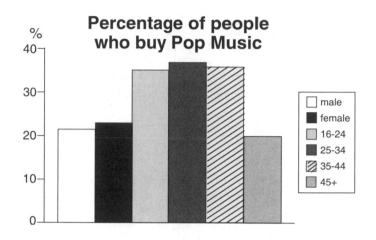

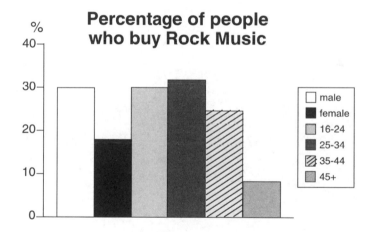

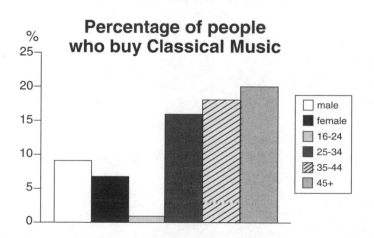

You should spend about 40 minutes on this task.

Present a written argument or case to an educated non-specialist audience on the following topic:

> *Some employers reward members of staff for their exceptional contribution to the company by giving them extra money. This practice can act as an incentive for some but may also have a negative impact on others.*
>
> *To what extent is this style of management effective?*
> *Are there better ways of encouraging employees to work hard?*

You should write at least 250 words.

You should use your own ideas, knowledge and experience and support your arguments with examples and relevant evidence.

Speaking module (11–14 minutes)

PART 1

The examiner will ask you questions about yourself, such as:

- ¥ *What's your name?*
- ¥ *What nationality are you?*
- ¥ *What part of your country do you come from?*
- ¥ *Can you describe your home town/village?*
- ¥ *What do you like doing in your free time? Why?*
- ¥ *Are there any new hobbies that you would like to take up? Why?*

PART 2

The topic for your talk will be written on a card which the examiner will hand you. Read it carefully, then make some brief notes.

A Competition

INSTRUCTIONS

Please read the topic below carefully. You will be asked to talk about it for 1 to 2 minutes.

You have one minute to think about what you're going to say.
You can make some notes to help you if you wish.

Describe a competition (or contest) that you have entered.

You should say: when the competition took place
what you had to do
how well you did it

Describe how you felt about the competition.

At the end of your talk, the examiner will ask one or two brief questions to signal that it is time to stop talking. For example, he or she might ask you:

Do you enjoy entering competitions?
Have you entered any other competitions?

PART 3

Once your talk in Part 2 is over, your examiner will ask you further questions related to the topic in Part 2. The exaimer may ask you to speak about these points.

Competition

- ¥ *competition at a young age*
- ¥ *competition at school*
- ¥ *value of international competitions*
- ¥ *the psychology of competing*
- ¥ *competitive spirit*

Listening module (30 minutes + transfer time)

Questions 1–10

Questions 1–4

Complete the form below.

*Write **NO MORE THAN THREE WORDS** or **A NUMBER** for each answer.*

Conference Registration Form

Example
Name of Conference: *Beyond 2000*

Name: Melanie **1** ....Ms......

Address: **2** Room .... at .... Newtown

Faculty: **3** ....

Student No: **4** ....

Questions 5–10

*Circle the correct letters **A–C**.*

Registration for:	5	A	Half day
		B	Full day
		C	Full conference
Accommodation required:	6	A	Share room/share bathroom
		B	Own room/share bathroom
		C	Own room with bathroom
Meals required:	7	A	Breakfast
		B	Lunch
		C	Dinner
Friday SIGs:	8	A	Computers in Education
		B	Teaching Reading
		C	The Gifted Child
Saturday SIGs:	9	A	Cultural Differences
		B	Music in the Curriculum
		C	Gender Issues
Method of payment:	10	A	Credit Card
		B	Cheque
		C	Cash

Questions 11–20

Complete the table below.

*Write **NO MORE THAN THREE WORDS** for each answer.*

Name of Beach	Location	Geographical Features	Other information
Bandela	1km from Bandela **11** ……………… ……………………	surrounded by **12** …………… …………………………..	safe for children/ non-swimmers
Da Porlata	east corner of island	area around beach is **13** …………… ……………………………..	can hire **14** …………….. and ……………..
San Gett	just past 'Tip of Caln'	**15** …………….. beach on island	check **16** ………. …………………. on beach in rough weather
Blanaka	**17** …………… corner	surrounded by **18** …………….. …………………………..	can go caving and diving
Dissidor	close to Blanaka	need to walk over **19** ………………	need to take some **20** …………….. and …………….

Questions 21–30

Complete the notes below.

*Write **NO MORE THAN THREE WORDS** or **A NUMBER** for each answer.*

Procedure for Bookshops

- Keep database of course/college details.

- In May, request **21** ……………………………… from lecturers.

- Categorise books as – essential reading

    22 ………………………………. reading

    – background reading

When ordering, refer to last year's **23** ………………………….. .

    – type of course

    – students' **24** ………………………….. .

    – own judgement

Procedure for Publishers

- Send **25** ……………………………… to course providers

- Use websites

- Compose personal **26** …………………………. to academic staff

- Send **27** ……………………………… to bookstores

Students

Main objective is to find books that are good **28** ………………………………. .

Also look for books that are **29** ……………….. and **30** …………………………. .

Questions 31–40

Question 31

Circle the correct letters A–C.

31 At the start of her talk Rebecca points out that new graduates can find it hard to

    A get the right work.

    B take sufficient breaks.

    C motivate themselves.

Questions 32–33

*Circle **TWO** letters A–E.*

Which **TWO** of the following does Rebecca say worry new artists?

A   earning enough money

B   moving to a new environment

C   competing with other artists

D   having their work criticised

E   getting their portfolios ready

Questions 34–35

Circle the correct letters A–C.

34 Rebecca decided to become an illustrator because it

    A afforded her greater objectivity as an artist.

    B offered her greater freedom of expression.

    C allowed her to get her work published.

35 When she had developed a portfolio of illustrations, Rebecca found publishers

    A more receptive to her work.

    B equally cautious about her work.

    C uninterested in her work.

Questions 36–40

Complete the notes below.

*Write **NO MORE THAN THREE WORDS** for each answer.*

Suggestions for Developing a Portfolio

Get some artwork printed in magazines by entering **36** ....

Also you can **37** .... and .... mock up book pages.

Make an effort to use a variety of artistic **38** ....

Aim for recognition by dividing work into distinct **39** ....

Possibly use **40** ....

Reading module (1 hour)

READING PASSAGE 1 *You should spend about 20 minutes on **Questions 1–13** which are based on Reading Passage 1 below.*

Indoor Pollution

Since the early eighties we have been only too aware of the devastating effects of large–scale environmental pollution. Such pollution is generally the result of poor government planning in many developing nations or the short-sighted, selfish policies of the already industrialised countries which encourage a minority of the world's population to squander the majority of its natural resources.

While events such as the deforestation of the Amazon jungle or the nuclear disaster in Chernobyl continue to receive high media exposure, as do acts of environmental sabotage, it must be remembered that not all pollution is on this grand scale. A large proportion of the world's pollution has its source much closer to home. The recent spillage of crude oil from an oil tanker accidentally discharging its cargo straight into Sydney Harbour not only caused serious damage to the harbour foreshores but also created severely toxic fumes which hung over the suburbs for days and left the angry residents wondering how such a disaster could have been allowed to happen.

Avoiding pollution can be a full-time job. Try not to inhale traffic fumes; keep away from chemical plants and building-sites; wear a mask when cycling. It is enough to make you want to stay at home. But that, according to a growing body of scientific evidence, would also be a bad idea. Research shows that levels of pollutants such as hazardous gases, particulate matter and other chemical 'nasties' are usually higher indoors than out, even in the most

polluted cities. Since the average American spends 18 hours indoors for every hour outside, it looks as though many environmentalists may be attacking the wrong target.

The latest study, conducted by two environmental engineers, Richard Corsi and Cynthia Howard-Reed, of the University of Texas in Austin, and published in *Environmental Science and Technology*, suggests that it is the process of keeping clean that may be making indoor pollution worse. The researchers found that baths, showers, dishwashers and washing machines can all be significant sources of indoor pollution, because they extract trace amounts of chemicals from the water that they use and transfer them to the air.

Nearly all public water supplies contain very low concentrations of toxic chemicals, most of

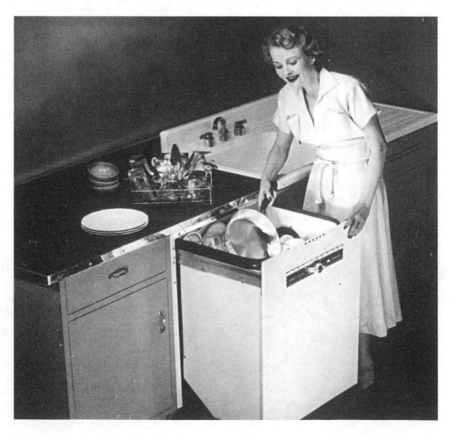

them left over from the otherwise beneficial process of chlorination. Dr. Corsi wondered whether they stay there when water is used, or whether they end up in the air that people breathe. The team conducted a series of experiments in which known quantities of five such chemicals were mixed with water and passed through a dishwasher, a washing machine, a shower head inside a shower stall or a tap in a bath, all inside a specially designed chamber. The levels of chemicals in the effluent water and in the air extracted from the chamber were then measured to see how much of each chemical had been transferred from the water into the air.

The degree to which the most volatile elements could be removed from the water, a process known as chemical stripping, depended on a wide range of factors, including the volatility of the chemical, the temperature of the water and the surface area available for transfer. Dishwashers were found to be particularly effective: the high-temperature spray, splashing against the crockery and cutlery, results in a nasty plume of toxic chemicals that escapes when the door is opened at the end of the cycle.

In fact, in many cases, the degree of exposure to toxic chemicals in tap water by inhalation is comparable to the exposure that would result from drinking the stuff. This is significant because many people are so concerned about water-borne pollutants that they drink only bottled water, worldwide sales of which are forecast to reach $72 billion by next year. D. Corsi's results suggest that they are being exposed to such pollutants anyway simply by breathing at home.

The aim of such research is not, however, to encourage the use of gas masks when unloading the washing. Instead, it is to bring a sense of perspective to the debate about pollution. According to Dr Corsi, disproportionate effort is wasted campaigning against certain forms of outdoor pollution, when there is as much or more cause for concern indoors, right under people's noses.

Using gas cookers or burning candles, for example, both result in indoor levels of carbon monoxide and particulate matter that are just as high as those to be found outside, amid heavy traffic. Overcrowded classrooms whose ventilation systems were designed for smaller numbers of children frequently contain levels of carbon dioxide that would be regarded as unacceptable on board a submarine. 'New car smell' is the result of high levels of toxic chemicals, not cleanliness. Laser printers, computers, carpets and paints all contribute to the noxious indoor mix.

The implications of indoor pollution for health are unclear. But before worrying about the problems caused by large-scale industry, it makes sense to consider the small-scale pollution at home and welcome international debate about this. Scientists investigating indoor pollution will gather next month in Edinburgh at the Indoor Air conference to discuss the problem. Perhaps unwisely, the meeting is being held indoors.

Questions 1–6

Choose the appropriate letters A–D and write them in boxes 1–6 on your answer sheet.

1   In the first paragraph, the writer argues that pollution

    A has increased since the eighties.

    B is at its worst in industrialised countries.

    C results from poor relations between nations.

    D is caused by human self-interest.

2   The Sydney Harbour oil spill was the result of a

    A ship refuelling in the harbour.

    B tanker pumping oil into the sea.

    C collision between two oil tankers.

    D deliberate act of sabotage.

3   In the 3rd paragraph the writer suggests that

    A people should avoid working in cities.

    B Americans spend too little time outdoors.

    C hazardous gases are concentrated in industrial suburbs.

    D there are several ways to avoid city pollution.

4   The Corsi research team hypothesised that

    A toxic chemicals can pass from air to water.

    B pollution is caused by dishwashers and baths.

    C city water contains insufficient chlorine.

    D household appliances are poorly designed.

5   As a result of their experiments, Dr Corsi's team found that

    A dishwashers are very efficient machines.

    B tap water is as polluted as bottled water.

    C indoor pollution rivals outdoor pollution.

    D gas masks are a useful protective device.

6   Regarding the dangers of pollution, the writer believes that

    A there is a need for rational discussion.

    B indoor pollution is a recent phenomenon.

    C people should worry most about their work environment.

    D industrial pollution causes specific diseases.

Questions 7–13

Reading Passage 1 describes a number of cause and effect relationships. Match each Cause (Questions 7–13) in List A with its Effect (A–J) in List B.

Write the appropriate letters (A–J) in boxes 7–13 on your answer sheet.

List A: CAUSES	**List B: EFFECTS**
7 Industrialised nations use a lot of energy.	**A** The focus of pollution moves to the home.
8 Oil spills into the sea.	**B** The levels of carbon monoxide rise.
9 The researchers publish their findings.	**C** The world's natural resources are unequally shared.
10 Water is brought to a high temperature.	**D** People demand an explanation.
11 People fear pollutants in tap water.	**E** Environmentalists look elsewhere for an explanation.
12 Air conditioning systems are inadequate.	**F** Chemicals are effectively stripped from the water.
13 Toxic chemicals are abundant in new cars.	**G** A clean odour is produced.
	H Sales of bottled water increase.
	I The levels of carbon dioxide rise.
	J The chlorine content of drinking water increased.

You should spend about 20 minutes on **Questions 14–27** *which are based on Reading Passage 2 below.*

Questions 14–19

*Reading Passage 2 has seven paragraphs **A–G**.*

From the list of headings below choose the most suitable heading for each paragraph.

*Write the appropriate numbers (**i–x**) in boxes 14–19 on your answer sheet.*

List of headings

i	Some success has resulted from observing how the brain functions.
ii	Are we expecting too much from one robot?
iii	Scientists are examining the humanistic possibilities.
iv	There are judgements that robots cannot make.
v	Has the power of robots become too great?
vi	Human skills have been heightened with the help of robotics.
vii	There are some things we prefer the brain to control.
viii	Robots have quietly infiltrated our lives.
ix	Original predictions have been revised.
x	Another approach meets the same result.

---

14   Paragraph A

15   Paragraph B

16   Paragraph C

17   Paragraph D

18   Paragraph E

19   Paragraph F

Example	*Answer*
Paragraph G	ii

ROBOTS

Since the dawn of human ingenuity, people have devised ever more cunning tools to cope with work that is dangerous, boring, onerous, or just plain nasty. That compulsion has culminated in robotics – the science of conferring various human capabilities on machines

A The modern world is increasingly populated by quasi-intelligent gizmos whose presence we barely notice but whose creeping ubiquity has removed much human drudgery. Our factories hum to the rhythm of robot assembly arms. Our banking is done at automated teller terminals that thank us with rote politeness for the transaction. Our subway trains are controlled by tireless robo-drivers. Our mine shafts are dug by automated moles, and our nuclear accidents – such as those at Three Mile Island and Chernobyl – are cleaned up by robotic muckers fit to withstand radiation.

Such is the scope of uses envisioned by Karel Capek, the Czech playwright who coined the term 'robot' in 1920 (the word 'robota' means 'forced labor' in Czech). As progress accelerates, the experimental becomes the exploitable at record pace.

B Other innovations promise to extend the abilities of human operators. Thanks to the incessant miniaturisation of electronics and micro-mechanics, there are already robot systems that can perform some kinds of brain and bone surgery with submillimeter accuracy – far greater precision than highly skilled physicians can achieve with their hands alone. At the same time, techniques of long-distance control will keep people even farther from hazard. In 1994 a ten-foot-tall NASA robotic explorer called Dante, with video-camera eyes and with spiderlike legs, scrambled over the menacing rim of an Alaskan volcano while technicians 2,000 miles away in California watched the scene by satellite and controlled Dante's descent.

C But if robots are to reach the next stage of labour-saving utility, they will have to operate with less human supervision and be able to make at least a few decisions for themselves – goals that pose a formidable challenge. 'While we know how to tell a robot to handle a specific error,' says one expert, 'we can't yet give a robot enough common sense to reliably interact with a dynamic world.' Indeed the quest for true artificial intelligence (AI) has produced very mixed results. Despite a spasm of initial optimism in the 1960s and 1970s, when it appeared that transistor circuits and microprocessors might be able to perform in the same way as the human brain by the 21st century, researchers lately have extended their forecasts by decades if not centuries.

D What they found, in attempting to model thought, is that the human brain's roughly one hundred billion neurons are much more talented – and human perception far more complicated – than previously imagined. They have built robots that can recognise the misalignment of a machine panel by a fraction of a millimeter in a controlled factory environment. But the human mind can glimpse a rapidly changing scene and immediately disregard the 98 per cent that is irrelevant, instantaneously focusing on the woodchuck at the side of a winding forest road or the single suspicious face in a tumultuous crowd. The most advanced computer systems on Earth can't approach that kind of ability, and neuroscientists still don't know quite how we do it.

E Nonetheless, as information theorists, neuroscientists, and computer experts pool their talents, they are finding ways to get some lifelike intelligence from robots. One method renounces the linear, logical structure of conventional electronic circuits in favour of the messy, ad hoc arrangement of a real brain's neurons. These 'neural networks' do not have to be programmed. They can 'teach' themselves by a system of feedback signals that reinforce electrical pathways that produced correct responses and, conversely, wipe out connections that produced errors. Eventually the net wires itself into a system that can pronounce certain words or distinguish certain shapes.

F In other areas researchers are struggling to fashion a more natural relationship between people and robots in the expectation that some day machines will take on some tasks now done by humans in, say, nursing homes. This is particularly important in Japan, where the percentage of elderly citizens is rapidly increasing. So experiments at the Science University of Tokyo have created a 'face robot' – a life-size, soft plastic model of a female head with a video camera imbedded in the left eye – as a prototype. The researchers' goal is to create robots that people feel comfortable around. They are concentrating on the face because they believe facial expressions are the most important way to transfer emotional messages. We read those messages by interpreting expressions to decide whether a person is happy, frightened, angry, or nervous. Thus the Japanese robot is designed to detect emotions in the person it is 'looking at' by sensing changes in the spatial arrangement of the person's eyes, nose, eyebrows, and mouth. It compares those configurations with a database of standard facial expressions and guesses the emotion. The robot then uses an ensemble of tiny pressure pads to adjust its plastic face into an appropriate emotional response.

G Other labs are taking a different approach, one that doesn't try to mimic human intelligence or emotions. Just as computer design has moved away from one central mainframe in favour of myriad individual workstations – and single processors have been replaced by arrays of smaller units that break a big problem into parts that are solved simultaneously – many experts are now investigating whether swarms of semi-smart robots can generate a collective intelligence that is greater than the sum of its parts. That's what beehives and ant colonies do, and several teams are betting that legions of mini-critters working together like an ant colony could be sent to explore the climate of planets or to inspect pipes in dangerous industrial situations.

Questions 20—24

Do the following statements agree with the information given in Reading Passage 2?

In boxes 20—24 on your answer sheet write

YES   *if the statement agrees with the information*
NO   *if the statement contradicts the information*
NOT GIVEN *if there is no information on this in the passage*

20   Karel Capek successfully predicted our current uses for robots.

21   Lives were saved by the NASA robot, Dante.

22   Robots are able to make fine visual judgements.

23   The internal workings of the brain can be replicated by robots.

24   The Japanese have the most advanced robot systems.

Questions 25—27

Complete the summary below with words taken from paragraph F.

*Use **NO MORE THAN THREE WORDS** for each answer.*

Write your answers in boxes 25—27 on your answer sheet.

The prototype of the Japanese face robot observes humans through a ... **25** ... which is planted in its head. It then refers to a ... **26** ... of typical looks that the human face can have, to decide what emotion the person is feeling. To respond to this expression, the robot alters its own expression using a number of ... **27** ... .

SAVING LANGUAGE

For the first time, linguists have put a price on language. To save a language from extinction isn't cheap – but more and more people are arguing that the alternative is the death of communities

There is nothing unusual about a single language dying. Communities have come and gone throughout history, and with them their language. But what is happening today is extraordinary, judged by the standards of the past. It is language extinction on a massive scale. According to the best estimates, there are some 6,000 languages in the world. Of these, about half are going to die out in the course of the next century: that's 3,000 languages in 1,200 months. On average, there is a language dying out somewhere in the world every two weeks or so.

How do we know? In the course of the past two or three decades, linguists all over the world have been gathering comparative data. If they find a language with just a few speakers left, and nobody is bothering to pass the language on to the children, they conclude that language is bound to die out soon. And we have to draw the same conclusion if a language has less than 100 speakers. It is not likely to last very long. A 1999 survey shows that 97 per cent of the world's languages are spoken by just four per cent of the people.

It is too late to do anything to help many languages, where the speakers are too few or too old, and where the community is too busy just trying to survive to care about their language. But many languages are not in such a serious position. Often, where languages are seriously endangered, there are things that can be done to give new life to them. It is called revitalisation.

Once a community realises that its language is in danger, it can start to introduce measures which can genuinely revitalise. The community itself

must want to save its language. The culture of which it is a part must need to have a respect for minority languages. There needs to be funding, to support courses, materials, and teachers. And there need to be linguists, to get on with the basic task of putting the language down on paper. That's the bottom line: getting the language documented – recorded, analysed, written down. People must be able to read and write if they and their language are to have a future in an increasingly computer-literate civilisation.

But can we save a few thousand languages, just like that? Yes, if the will and funding were available. It is not cheap, getting linguists into the field, training local analysts, supporting the community with language resources and teachers, compiling grammars and dictionaries, writing materials for use in schools. It takes time, lots of it, to revitalise an endangered language. Conditions vary so much that it is difficult to generalise, but a figure of $100,000 a year per language cannot be far from the truth. If we devoted that amount of effort over three years for each of 3,000 languages, we would be talking about some $900 million.

There are some famous cases which illustrate what can be done. Welsh, alone among the Celtic languages, is not only stopping its steady decline towards extinction but showing signs of real growth. Two Language Acts protect the status of Welsh now, and its presence is increasingly in evidence wherever you travel in Wales.

On the other side of the world, Maori in New Zealand has been maintained by a system of so-called 'language nests', first introduced in 1982. These are organisations which provide children under five with a domestic setting in which they are intensively exposed to the language. The staff are all Maori speakers from the local community. The hope is that the children will keep their Maori skills alive after leaving the nests, and that as they grow older they will in turn become role models to a new generation of young children. There are cases like this all over the world. And when the reviving language is associated with a degree of political autonomy, the growth can be especially striking, as shown by Faroese, spoken in the Faroe Islands, after the islanders received a measure of autonomy from Denmark.

In Switzerland, Romansch was facing a difficult situation, spoken in five very different dialects, with small and diminishing numbers, as young people left their community for work in the German-speaking cities. The solution here was the creation in the 1980s of a unified written language for all these dialects. Romansch Grischun, as it is now called, has official status in parts of Switzerland, and is being increasingly used in spoken form on radio and television.

A language can be brought back from the very brink of extinction. The Ainu language of Japan, after many years of neglect and repression, had reached a stage where there were only eight fluent speakers left, all elderly. However, new government policies brought fresh attitudes and a positive interest in survival. Several 'semi-speakers' – people who had become unwilling to speak Ainu because of the negative attitudes by Japanese speakers – were prompted to become active speakers again. There is fresh interest now and the language is more publicly available than it has been for years.

If good descriptions and materials are available, even extinct languages can be resurrected. Kaurna, from South Australia, is an example. This language had been extinct for about a century, but had been quite well documented. So, when a strong movement grew for its revival, it was possible to reconstruct it. The revised language is not the same as the original, of course. It lacks the range that the original had, and much of the old vocabulary. But it can nonetheless act as a badge of present-day identity for its people. And as long as people continue to value it as a true marker of their identity, and are prepared to keep using it, it will develop new functions and new vocabulary, as any other living language would do.

It is too soon to predict the future of these revived languages, but in some parts of the world they are attracting precisely the range of positive attitudes and grass roots support which are the preconditions for language survival. In such unexpected but heart-warming ways might we see the grand total of languages in the world minimally increased.

Questions 28–32

Do the following statements agree with the views of the writer in Reading Passage 3?

In boxes 28–32 on your answer sheet write

YES *if the statement agrees with the writer's views*
NO *if the statement contradicts the writer's views*
NOT GIVEN *if it is impossible to say what the writer thinks about this*

28 The rate at which languages are becoming extinct has increased.

29 Research on the subject of language extinction began in the 1990s.

30 In order to survive, a language needs to be spoken by more than 100 people.

31 Certain parts of the world are more vulnerable than others to language extinction.

32 Saving language should be the major concern of any small community whose language is under threat.

Questions 33–35

The list below gives some of the factors that are necessary to assist the revitalisation of a language within a community.

*Which **THREE** of the factors are mentioned by the writer of the text?*

*Write the appropriate letters **A–G** in boxes 33–35 on your answer sheet.*

A the existence of related languages

B support from the indigenous population

C books tracing the historical development of the language

D on-the-spot help from language experts

E a range of speakers of different ages

F formal education procedures

G a common purpose for which the language is required

*Match the languages **A–F** with the statements below (Questions 36–40) which describe how a language was saved.*

Write your answers in boxes 36–40 on your answer sheet.

Languages		
A Welsh	**D**	Romansch
B Maori	**E**	Ainu
C Faroese	**F**	Kaurna

36 The region in which the language was spoken gained increased independence.

37 People were encouraged to view the language with less prejudice.

38 Language immersion programmes were set up for sectors of the population.

39 A merger of different varieties of the language took place.

40 Written samples of the language permitted its revitalisation.

Writing module (1 hour)

You should spend about 20 minutes on this task.

The graphs below show the number of men and women in full and part-time employment in Australia between 1973 and 1993.

Write a report for a university lecturer describing the information shown below.

You should write at least 150 words.

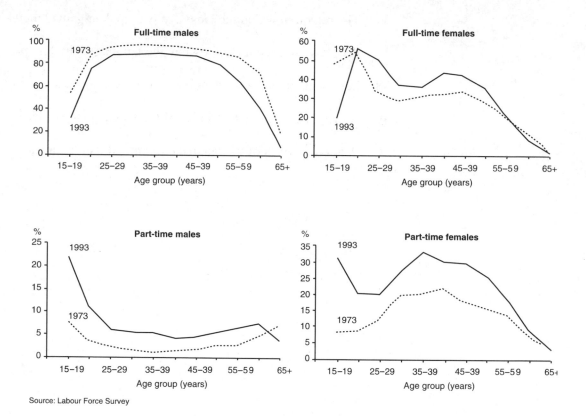

Source: Labour Force Survey

You should spend about 40 minutes on this task.

Present a written argument or case to an educated non-specialist audience on the following topic:

> *In the past, sporting champions used to be motivated primarily by the desire to win a match or to break world records. These days, they are more likely to be motivated by prize money and the opportunity to be famous.*
>
> *What message does this send to young people and how does this attitude to sport affect the sports themselves?*
>
> *Give reasons for your answers.*

You should write at least 250 words.

You should use your own ideas, knowledge and experience and support your arguments with examples and relevant evidence.

Speaking module (11–14 minutes)

PART 1

The examiner will ask you some questions about yourself, such as:

¥ *What country do you come from?*

¥ *Which other countries have you visited?*

¥ *Are there any countries you would like to visit? Why?*

¥ *What do you find difficult about travelling?*

¥ *What do you enjoy about travelling?*

¥ *What is your preferred method of travel?*

PART 2

The topic for your talk will be written on a card which the examiner will hand you. Read it carefully and then make some brief notes.

> **A job you have done**
>
> > INSTRUCTIONS
> > Please read the topic below carefully. You will be asked to talk about it for 1 to 2 minutes.
> >
> > You have one minute to think about what you re going to say.
> > You can make some notes to help you if you wish.
>
> Describe a job that you have done.
>
> You should say: how you got the job
>
> what the job involved
>
> how long the job lasted
>
> Describe how well you did the job.

At the end of your talk, the examiner will ask one or two brief questions to signal that it is time to stop talking. For example, he or she might ask you:

Do you value the experience you had in this job?
Would you consider doing the same type of job again?

PART 3

Once your talk in Part 2 is over, your examiner will ask you further questions related to the topic in Part 2. The examiner may ask you to speak about these points.

A job you have done

¥ *advantages of young people working*   ¥ *motivating people to work*

¥ *types of part-time work*   ¥ *job security -vs- having more than one career*

¥ *choosing a career*

TEST 4

Listening module (30 minutes + transfer time)

Questions 1–10

Complete the notes below.

*Write **NO MORE THAN THREE WORDS** or **A NUMBER** for each answer.*

Event Details

Type of event: *Example*   **Dragon Boat Race**

Race details

Day & date: **1** ………………….……………..

Place: Brighton **2** …………….…………..

Registration time: **3** ……………..………..

Sponsorship

- aim to raise over **4** …………….…………….. as a team and get a free t-shirt

- free Prize Draw for trip to **5** ………………………………………..

Team details

- must have crew of 20 and elect a **6** ………………….……………..

- under 18s need to have **7** ……………….……… to enter

- need to hire **8** …………………………………….

- advised to bring extra **9** ………….……………..

- must choose a **10** …………………….………… for the team

Questions 11–20

Questions 11–15

Complete the notes below.

Use NO MORE THAN THREE WORDS for each answer.

KIWI FACT SHEET

Pictures of kiwis are found on **11** .... and ....

The name 'kiwi' comes from its **12** ....

The kiwi has poor sight but a good **13** ....

Kiwis cannot **14** ....

Kiwis are endangered by **15** '... ,

Questions 16–17

Complete the notes below.

Use NO MORE THAN THREE WORDS for each answer.

Kiwi Recovery Program

Stage of program	Program involves
(16)	Looking at kiwi survival needs
Action	Putting science into practice
(17)	Schools and the website

Questions 18–20

Complete the flow chart below.

*Use **NO MORE THAN THREE WORDS** or **A NUMBER** for each answer.*

OPERATION NEST EGG

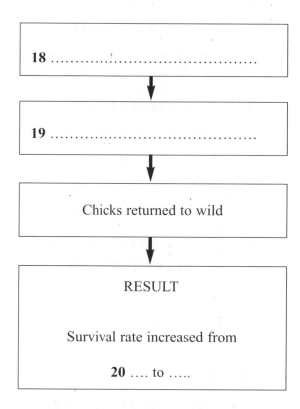

18 ....

↓

19 ....

↓

Chicks returned to wild

↓

RESULT

Survival rate increased from

20 .... to .....

Questions 21–30

Questions 21–24

Circle the correct letters A–C.

21 The professor says that super highways
   A lead to better lifestyles.

   B are a feature of wealthy cities.

   C result in more city suburbs.

22 The student thinks people
   A like the advantages of the suburbs.

   B rarely go into the city for entertainment.

   C enjoy living in the city.

23 The professor suggests that in five years' time
   A City Link will be choked by traffic.

   B public transport will be more popular.

   C roads will cost ten times more to build.

24 The student believes that highways
   A encourage a higher standard of driving.

   B result in lower levels of pollution.

   C discourage the use of old cars.

Questions 25–26

Label the two bars identified on the graph below.

Choose your answers from the box and write them next to Questions 25–26.

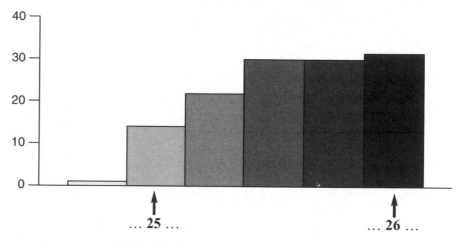

Percentage of people using public transport by capital city

List of cities:	Detroit
	Frankfurt
	London
	Paris
	Sydney
	Toronto

Questions 27–28

*Circle **TWO** letters **A–F**.*

Which **TWO** facts are mentioned about Copenhagen?

A   live street theatre encouraged

B   30% of citizens walk to work

C   introduction of parking metres

D   annual reduction of parking spots

E   free city bicycles

F   free public transport

Questions 29–30

*Circle **TWO** letters **A–F**.*

Which **TWO** reasons are given for the low popularity of public transport?

A   buses slower than cars

B   low use means reduced service

C   private cars safer

D   public transport expensive

E   frequent stopping inconvenient

F   making connections takes time

Questions 31–40

Questions 31–32

Complete the notes below.

Write **NO MORE THAN THREE WORDS** *for each answer.*

Reasons for preserving food
• Available all year
• For **31** ....
• In case of **32** ....

Questions 33–37

Complete the table below.

Write **NO MORE THAN THREE WORDS** *for each answer.*

Method of preservation	Advantage	Disadvantage
Ultra-high temperature (UHT milk)	... **33** ...	spoils the taste
canning	inexpensive	risk of ... **34** ...
refrigeration	stays fresh without processing	requires ... **35** ...
... **36** ...	effective	time-consuming.
drying	long-lasting, light and ... **37** ...	loses nutritional value

Tip Strip

Questions 38–40: Look carefully at the diagram to make sure you understand what needs to be labelled. Look at Question 40: Will you need to label an actual part of the machine or something that will come out of the machine?

• Note that the numbers go in a clockwise direction round the diagram.

• Notice the title of the diagram. Make sure you listen out for any signpost words indicating that the speaker is now going to talk about the diagram.

• Do not take the words from the title for your answer as they will not be correct.

Questions 38–40

Label the diagram.

*Write **NO MORE THAN THREE WORDS** for each answer.*

Roller drying

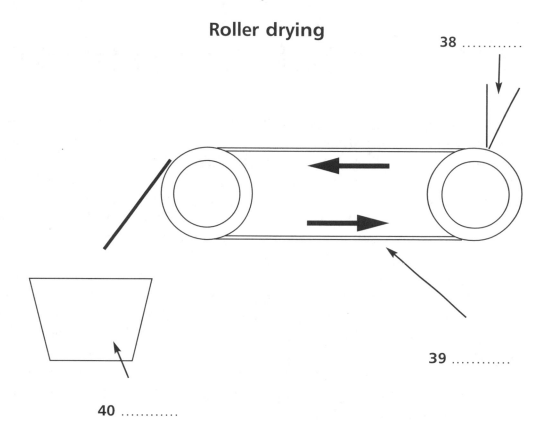

38 ....

39 ....

40 ....

*You should spend about 20 minutes on **Questions 1–13** which are based on the Reading Passage below.*

The Great Australian Fence

A war has been going on for almost a hundred years between the sheep farmers of Australia and the dingo, Australia's wild dog. To protect their livelihood, the farmers built a wire fence, 3,307 miles of continuous wire mesh, reaching from the coast of South Australia all the way to the cotton fields of eastern Queensland, just short of the Pacific Ocean.

The Fence is Australia's version of the Great Wall of China, but even longer, erected to keep out hostile invaders, in this case hordes of yellow dogs. The empire it preserves is that of the woolgrowers, sovereigns of the world's second largest sheep flock, after China's – some 123 million head – and keepers of a wool export business worth four billion dollars. Never mind that more and more people – conservationists, politicians, taxpayers and animal lovers – say that such a barrier would never be allowed today on ecological grounds. With sections of it almost a hundred years old, the dog fence has become, as conservationist Lindsay Fairweather ruefully admits, 'an icon of Australian frontier ingenuity'.

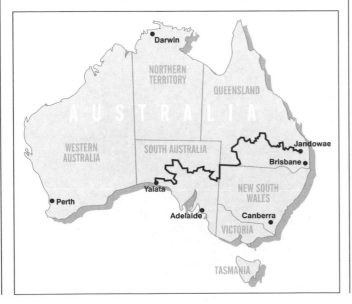

To appreciate this unusual outback monument and to meet the people whose livelihoods depend on it, I spent part of an Australian autumn travelling the wire. It's known by different names in different states: the Dog Fence in South Australia, the Border Fence in New South Wales and the Barrier Fence in Queensland. I would call it simply the Fence.

For most of its prodigious length, this epic fence winds like a river across a landscape that, unless a big rain has fallen, scarcely has rivers. The eccentric route, prescribed mostly by property lines, provides a sampler of outback topography: the Fence goes over sand dunes, past salt lakes, up and down rock-strewn hills, through dense scrub and across barren plains.

The Fence stays away from towns. Where it passes near a town, it has actually become a tourist attraction visited on bus tours. It marks the traditional dividing line between cattle and sheep. Inside, where the dingoes are legally classified as vermin, they are shot, poisoned and trapped. Sheep and dingoes do not mix and the Fence sends that message mile after mile.

What is this creature that by itself threatens an entire industry, inflicting several millions of dollars of damage a year despite the presence of the world's most obsessive fence? Cousin to the coyote and the jackal, descended from the Asian wolf, *Canis lupus dingo* is an introduced species of wild dog. Skeletal remains indicate that the dingo was introduced to Australia more than 3,500 years ago probably with Asian seafarers who landed on the north coast. The adaptable dingo spread rapidly and in a short time became the top predator, killing off all its marsupial competitors. The dingo looks like a small wolf with a long nose, short pointed ears and a bushy tail. Dingoes rarely bark; they yelp and howl. Standing about 22 inches at the shoulder – slightly taller than a coyote – the dingo is Australia's largest land carnivore.

The woolgrowers' war against dingoes, which is similar to the sheep ranchers' rage against coyotes in the US, started not long after the first European settlers disembarked in 1788, bringing with them a cargo of sheep. Dingoes officially became outlaws in 1830 when governments placed a bounty on their heads. Today bounties for problem dogs killing sheep inside the Fence can reach $500. As pioneers penetrated the interior with their flocks of sheep, fences replaced shepherds until, by the end of the 19th century, thousands of miles of barrier fencing crisscrossed the vast grazing lands.

'The dingo started out as a quiet observer,' writes Roland Breckwoldt, in *A Very Elegant Animal: The Dingo,* 'but soon came to represent everything that was dark and dangerous on the continent.' It is estimated that since sheep arrived in Australia, dingo numbers have increased a hundredfold. Though dingoes have been eradicated from parts of Australia, an educated guess puts the population at more than a million.

Eventually government officials and graziers agreed that one well-maintained fence, placed on the outer rim of sheep country and paid for by taxes levied on woolgrowers, should supplant the maze of private netting. By 1960, three states joined their barriers to form a single dog fence.

The intense private battles between woolgrowers and dingoes have usually served to define the Fence only in economic terms. It marks the difference between profit and loss. Yet the Fence casts a much broader ecological shadow for it has become a kind of terrestrial dam, deflecting the flow of animals inside and out. The ecological side effects appear most vividly at Sturt National Park. In 1845, explorer Charles Sturt led an expedition through these parts on a futile search for an inland sea. For Sturt and other early explorers, it was a rare event to see a kangaroo. Now they are ubiquitous for without a native predator the kangaroo population has exploded inside the Fence. Kangaroos are now cursed more than dingoes. They have become the rivals of sheep, competing for water and grass. In response state governments cull* more than three million kangaroos a year to keep Australia's national symbol from overrunning the pastoral lands. Park officials, who recognise that the fence is to blame, respond to the excess of kangaroos by saying 'The fence is there, and we have to live with it.'

*Cull = to kill animals to reduce their population.

Questions 1–4

*Choose the appropriate letters **A–D** and write them in boxes 1–4 on your answer sheet.*

1 Why was the fence built?

    A to separate the sheep from the cattle

    B to stop the dingoes from being slaughtered by farmers

    C to act as a boundary between properties

    D to protect the Australian wool industry

2 On what point do the conservationists and politicians agree?

    A Wool exports are vital to the economy.

    B The fence poses a threat to the environment.

    C The fence acts as a useful frontier between states.

    D The number of dogs needs to be reduced.

3 Why did the author visit Australia?

    A to study Australian farming methods

    B to investigate how the fence was constructed

    C because he was interested in life around the fence

    D because he wanted to learn more about the wool industry

4 How does the author feel about the fence?

    A impressed

    B delighted

    C shocked

    D annoyed

Questions 5–11

Do the following statements agree with the information given in Reading Passage 1?

In boxes 5–11 on your answer sheet write

YES   *if the statement agrees with the information*
NO   *if the statement contradicts the information*
NOT GIVEN *if there is no information on this in the passage*

5   The fence serves a different purpose in each state.

6   The fence is only partially successful.

7   The dingo is indigenous to Australia.

8   Dingoes have flourished as a result of the sheep industry.

9   Dingoes are known to attack humans.

10   Kangaroos have increased in number because of the fence.

11   The author does not agree with the culling of kangaroos.

Questions 12–13

*Choose the appropriate letters **A–D** and write them in boxes 12–13 on your answer sheet.*

12   When did the authorities first acknowledge the dingo problem?

   A 1788

   B 1830

   C 1845

   D 1960

13   How do the park officials feel about the fence?

   A philosophical

   B angry

   C pleased

   D proud

IT'S ECO-LOGICAL

Planning an eco-friendly holiday can be a minefield for the well-meaning traveller, says Steve Watkins. But help is now at hand

If there were awards for tourism phrases that have been hijacked, diluted and misused then 'ecotourism' would earn top prize. The term first surfaced in the early 1980s reflecting a surge in environmental awareness and a realisation by tour operators that many travellers wanted to believe their presence abroad would not have a negative impact. It rapidly became the hottest marketing tag a holiday could carry.

These days the ecotourism label is used to cover anything from a two-week tour living with remote Indonesian tribes, to a one-hour motorboat trip through an Australian gorge. In fact, any tour that involves cultural interaction, natural beauty spots, wildlife or a dash of soft adventure is likely to be included in the overflowing ecotourism folder. There is no doubt the original motives behind the movement were honourable attempts to provide a way for those who cared to make informed choices, but the lack of regulations and a standard industry definition left many travellers lost in an ecotourism jungle.

It is easier to understand why the ecotourism market has become so overcrowded when we look at its wider role in the world economy. According to World Tourism Organisation figures, ecotourism is worth US$20 billion a year and makes up one-fifth of all international tourism. Add to this an annual growth rate of around five per cent and the pressure for many operators, both in developed and developing countries, to jump on the accelerating bandwagon is compelling. Without any widely recognised accreditation system, the consumer has been left to investigate the credentials of an operator themselves. This is a time-consuming process and many travellers usually take an operator's claims at face value, only adding to the proliferation of fake ecotours.

However, there are several simple questions that will provide qualifying evidence of a company's commitment to minimise its impact on the environment and maximise the benefits to the tourism area's local community. For example, does the company use recycled or sustainable, locally harvested materials to build its tourist properties? Do they pay fair wages to all employees? Do they offer training to employees? It is common for city entrepreneurs to own tour companies in country areas, which can mean the money you pay ends up in the city rather than in the community being visited. By taking a little extra time to investigate the ecotourism options, it is not only possible to guide your custom to worthy operators but you will often find that the experience they offer is far more rewarding.

The ecotourism business is still very much in need of a shake-up and a standardised approach. There are a few organisations that have sprung up in the last ten years or so that endeavour to educate travellers and operators about the benefits of responsible ecotourism. Founded in 1990, the Ecotourism Society (TES) is a non-profit organisation of travel industry, conservation and ecological professionals, which aims to make ecotourism a genuine tool for conservation and sustainable development. Helping to create inherent economic value in wilderness environments and threatened cultures has undoubtedly been one of the ecotourism movement's most notable achievements. TES organises an annual initiative to further aid development of the ecotourism industry. This year it is launching 'Your Travel Choice Makes a Difference', an educational campaign aimed at helping consumers understand the potential positive and negative impacts of their travel decisions. TES also offers guidance on the choice of ecotour and has established a register of approved ecotourism operators around the world.

A leading ecotourism operator in the United Kingdom is Tribes, which won the 1999 Tourism Concern and Independent Traveller's World 'Award for Most Responsible Tour Operator'. Amanda Marks, owner and director of Tribes, believes that the ecotourism industry still has some way to go to get its house in order. Until now, no ecotourism accreditation scheme has really worked, principally because there has been no systematic way of checking that accredited companies actually comply with the code of practice. Amanda believes that the most promising system is the recently re-launched Green Globe 21 scheme. The Green Globe 21 award is based on the sustainable development standards contained in Agenda 21 from the 1992 Earth Summit and was originally coordinated by the World Travel & Tourism Council (WTTC). The scheme is now an independent concern, though the WTTC still supports it. Until recently, tour companies became affiliates and could use the Green Globe logo merely on payment of an annual fee, hardly a suitable qualifying standard. However, in November 1999 Green Globe 21 introduced an annual, independent check on operators wishing to use the logo.

Miriam Cain, from the Green Globe 21 marketing development, explains that current and new affiliates will now have one year to ensure that their operations comply with Agenda 21 standards. If they fail the first inspection, they can only reapply once. The inspection process is not a cheap option, especially for large companies, but the benefits of having Green Globe status and the potential operational cost savings that complying with the standards can bring should be significant. 'We have joint ventures with organisations around the world, including Australia and the Caribbean, that will allow us to effectively check all affiliate operators,' says Miriam. The scheme also allows destination communities to become Green Globe 21 approved.

For a relatively new industry it is not surprising that ecotourism has undergone teething pains. However, there are signs that things are changing for the better. With a committed and unified approach by the travel industry, local communities, travellers and environmental experts could make ecotourism a tag to be proud of and trusted.

Questions 14–19

Do the following statements agree with the views of the writer in Reading Passage 2?

In boxes 14–19 on your answer sheet write

YES   *if the statement agrees with the writer's views*
NO   *if the statement contradicts the writer's views*
NOT GIVEN   *if it is impossible to say what the writer thinks about this*

14   The term 'ecotourism' has become an advertising gimmick.

15   The intentions of those who coined the term 'ecotourism' were sincere.

16   Ecotourism is growing at a faster rate than any other type of travel.

17   It is surprising that so many tour organisations decided to become involved in ecotourism.

18   Tourists have learnt to make investigations about tour operators before using them.

19   Tourists have had bad experiences on ecotour holidays.

Questions 20–22

*According to the information given in the reading passage, which **THREE** of the following are true of the Ecotourism Society (TES)?*

*Write the appropriate letters **A–F** in boxes 20–22 on your answer sheet.*

A   It has monitored the growth in ecotourism.

B   It involves a range of specialists in the field.

C   It has received public recognition for the role it performs.

D   It sets up regular ecotour promotions.

E   It offers information on ecotours at an international level.

F   It consults with people working in tourist destinations

Questions 23–24

*According to the information given in the reading passage, which **TWO** of the following are true of the Green Globe 21 award?*

*Write the appropriate letters **A–D** in boxes 23–24 on your answer sheet.*

A   The scheme is self-regulating.

B   Amanda Marks was recruited to develop the award.

C   Prior to 1999 companies were not required to pay for membership.

D   Both tour operators and tour sites can apply for affiliation.

E   It intends to reduce the number of ecotour operators.

Questions 25–27

*Using **NO MORE THAN THREE WORDS**, answer the following questions.*

Write your answers in boxes 25–27 on your answer sheet.

25   Which body provides information on global tourist numbers?

26   Who often gains financially from tourism in rural environments?

27   Which meeting provided the principles behind the Green Globe 21 regulations?

READING PASSAGE 3

You should spend about 20 minutes on **Questions 28–40** which are based on Reading Passage 3 below.

Striking the RIGHT NOTE

Is perfect pitch a rare talent possessed solely by the likes of Beethoven? Kathryn Brown discusses this much sought-after musical ability

The uncanny, if sometimes distracting, ability to name a solitary note out of the blue, without any other notes for reference, is a prized musical talent – and a scientific mystery. Musicians with perfect pitch – or, as many researchers prefer to call it, absolute pitch – can often play pieces by ear, and many can transcribe music brilliantly. That's because they perceive the position of a note in the musical stave – its pitch – as clearly as the fact that they heard it. Hearing and naming the pitch go hand in hand.

By contrast, most musicians follow not the notes, but the relationship between them. They may easily recognise two notes as being a certain number of tones apart, but could name the higher note as an E only if they are told the lower one is a C, for example. This is relative pitch. Useful, but much less mysterious.

For centuries, absolute pitch has been thought of as the preserve of the musical elite. Some estimates suggest that maybe fewer than 1 in 2,000 people possess it. But a growing number of studies, from speech experiments to brain scans, are now suggesting that a knack for absolute pitch may be far more common, and more varied, than previously thought. 'Absolute pitch is not an all or nothing feature,' says Marvin, a music theorist at the University of Rochester in New York state. Some researchers even claim that we could all develop the skill, regardless of our musical talent. And their work may finally settle a decades-old debate about whether absolute pitch depends on melodious genes – or early music lessons.

Music psychologist Diana Deutsch at the University of California in San Diego is the leading voice. Last month at the Acoustical Society of America meeting in Columbus, Ohio, Deutsch reported a study that suggests we all have the potential to acquire absolute pitch – and that speakers of tone languages use it every day. A third of the world's population – chiefly people in Asia and Africa – speak tone languages, in which a word's meaning can vary depending on the pitch a speaker uses.

Deutsch and her colleagues asked seven native Vietnamese speakers and 15 native Mandarin speakers to read out lists of words on different days. The chosen words spanned a range of pitches, to force the speakers to raise and lower their voices considerably. By recording these recited lists and taking the average pitch for each whole word, the researchers compared the pitches used by each person to say each word on different days.

Both groups showed strikingly consistent pitch for any given word – often less than a quarter-tone difference between days. 'The similarity,' Deutsch says, 'is mind-boggling.' It's also, she says, a real example of absolute pitch. As babies, the speakers learnt to associate certain pitches with meaningful words – just as a musician labels one tone A and another B – and they demonstrate this precise use of pitch regardless of whether or not they have had any musical training, she adds.

Deutsch isn't the only researcher turning up everyday evidence of absolute pitch. At least three other experiments have found that people can launch into familiar songs at or very near the correct pitches. Some researchers have nicknamed this ability 'absolute memory', and they say it pops up on other senses, too. Given studies like these, the real mystery is why we don't all have absolute pitch, says cognitive psychologist Daniel Levitin of McGill University in Montreal.

Over the past decade, researchers have confirmed that absolute pitch often runs in families. Nelson Freimer of the University of California in San Francisco, for example, is just completing a study that he says strongly suggests the right genes help create this brand of musical genius. Freimer gave tone tests to people with absolute pitch and to their relatives. He also tested several hundred other people who had taken early music lessons. He found that relatives of people with absolute pitch were far more likely to develop the skill than people who simply had the music lessons. 'There is clearly a familial aggregation of absolute pitch,' Freimer says.

Freimer says some children are probably genetically predisposed toward absolute pitch – and this innate inclination blossoms during childhood music lessons. Indeed, many researchers now point to this harmony of nature and nurture to explain why musicians with absolute pitch show different levels of the talent.

Indeed, researchers are finding more and more evidence suggesting music lessons are critical to the development of absolute pitch. In a survey of 2,700 students in American music conservatories and college programmes, New York University geneticist Peter Gregersen and his colleagues found that a whopping 32 per cent of the Asian students reported having absolute pitch, compared with just 7 per cent of non-Asian students. While that might suggest a genetic tendency towards absolute pitch in the Asian population, Gregersen says that the type and timing of music lessons probably explains much of the difference.

For one thing, those with absolute pitch started lessons, on average, when they were five years old, while those without absolute pitch started around the age of eight. Moreover, adds Gregersen, the type of music lessons favoured in Asia, and by many of the Asian families in his study, such as the Suzuki method, often focus on playing by ear and learning the names of musical notes, while those more commonly used in the US tend to emphasise learning scales in a relative pitch way. In Japanese pre-school music programmes, he says, children often have to listen to notes played on a piano and hold up a coloured flag to signal the pitch. 'There's a distinct cultural difference,' he says.

Deutsch predicts that further studies will reveal absolute pitch – in its imperfect, latent form – inside all of us. The Western emphasis on relative pitch simply obscures it, she contends. 'It's very likely that scientists will end up concluding that we're all born with the potential to acquire very fine-grained absolute pitch. It's really just a matter of life getting in the way.'

Questions 28–35

Complete the notes below using words from the box. Write your answers in boxes 28–35 on your answer sheet.

NOTES

Research is being conducted into the mysterious musical … **28** … some people possess known as perfect pitch. Musicians with this talent are able to name and sing a … **29** … without reference to another and it is this that separates them from the majority who have only … **30** … pitch. The research aims to find out whether this skill is the product of genetic inheritance or early exposure to … **31** … or, as some researchers believe, a combination of both. One research team sought a link between perfect pitch and … **32** … languages in order to explain the high number of Asian speakers with perfect pitch. Speakers of Vietnamese and Mandarin were asked to recite … **33** … on different occasions and the results were then compared in terms of … **34** … . A separate study found that the approach to teaching music in many Asian … **35** … emphasised playing by ear whereas the US method was based on the relative pitch approach.

List of Words

tendency	note	cultures	ability
song	ancient	pitch	learning scales
relative	primitive	absolute	spoken
music lessons	language	melody	names
tone	words	universities	musical instruments

Questions 36–40

Reading Passage 3 contains a number of opinions provided by five different scientists. Match each opinion (Questions 36–40) with one of the scientists (A–E).

Write your answers in boxes 36–40 on your answer sheet.

You may use any of the people A–E more than once.

A	Levitin
B	Deutsch
C	Gregersen
D	Marvin
E	Freimer

36 Absolute pitch is not a clear-cut issue.

37 Anyone can learn how to acquire perfect pitch.

38 It's actually surprising that not everyone has absolute pitch.

39 The perfect pitch ability is genetic.

40 The important thing is the age at which music lessons are started.

Writing module (1 hour)

You should spend about 20 minutes on this task.

The diagrams below show the development of the horse over a period of 40 million years.

Write a report for a university lecturer describing the information shown below.

You should write at least 150 words.

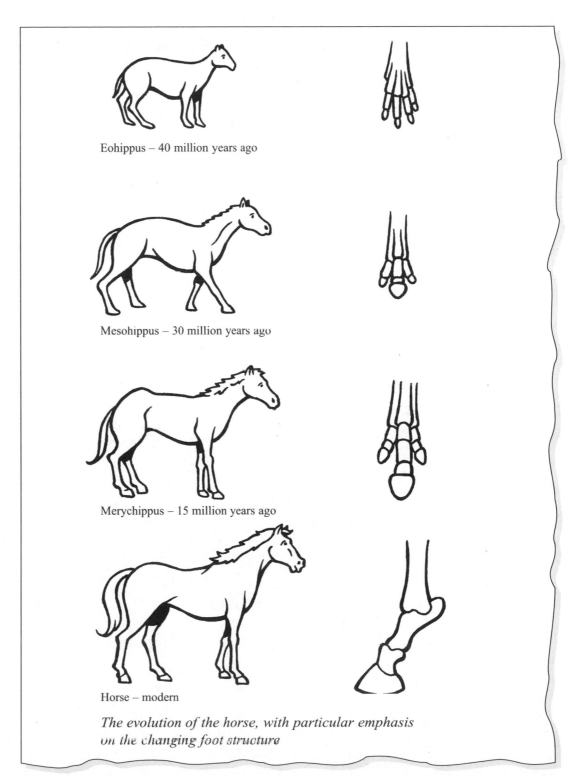

Eohippus – 40 million years ago

Mesohippus – 30 million years ago

Merychippus – 15 million years ago

Horse – modern

The evolution of the horse, with particular emphasis on the changing foot structure

You should spend about 40 minutes on this task.

Present a written argument or case to an educated non-specialist audience on the following topic:

> *'Failure is proof that the desire wasn't strong enough.'*
>
> *To what extent do you agree with this statement? Give reasons for your answer.*

You should write at least 250 words.

You should use your own ideas, knowledge and experience and support your arguments with examples and relevant evidence.

Speaking module (11–14 minutes)

PART 1 The examiner will ask you some questions about yourself, such as:

¥ *What town or city do you come from?*

¥ *Can you describe your family home?*

¥ *What does your family usually do at the weekend?*

¥ *Do you like going out with your family? Why?*

¥ *Where would you like to take a holiday? Why?*

¥ *Who would you most like to go on holiday with?*

¥ *What was the best holiday you ve ever had?*

PART 2 The topic for your talk will be written on a card which the examiner will hand you. Read it carefully and then make some brief notes.

A museum you have visited

> INSTRUCTIONS
>
> Please read the topic below carefully. You will be asked to talk about it for 1 to 2 minutes.
>
> You have one minute to think about what you re going to say.
>
> You can make some notes to help you if you wish.

Describe a museum or art gallery that you have visited.

You should say: where it is

                  why you went there

                  what you particularly remember about the place

---

At the end of your talk, the examiner will ask one or two brief questions to signal that it is time to stop talking. For examplc, he or she might ask you:

Do you like museums/art galleries?
Would you recommend this one to other people?

PART 3 Once your talk in Part 2 is over, your examiner will ask you further questions related to the topic in Part 2. The examiner may ask you to speak about these points.

Museums

¥ *the need for museums and art galleries in our society*

¥ *making museums more interesting*

¥ *museum art -vs- popular art*

¥ *graffiti* — art or vandalism?*

¥ *the role of public artworks, e.g. statues and buildings*

[*drawings made with spray paint in public spaces]

TEST 5

Listening module (30 minutes + transfer time)

Questions 1–10

Questions 1–6

Complete the form below.

*Write **NO MORE THAN THREE WORDS** or **A NUMBER** for each answer.*

Millennium Office Supplies
CUSTOMER ORDER FORM

Example:
ORDER PLACED BY .... *John Carter* ......

ACCOUNT NUMBER	1 ....
COMPANY NAME	2 ....

Envelopes
Size   **A4 normal**
Colour   3 ....
Quantity   4 ....
Photocopy paper
Colour   5 ....
Quantity   6 ....

Questions 7–9

*List **THREE** additional things that the man requests.*

*Write **NO MORE THAN THREE WORDS** for each answer.*

7 ....

8 ....

9 ....

Question 10

*Complete the notes. Write **NO MORE THAN THREE WORDS** for your answer.*

Special instructions: *Deliver goods* **10** ....

Questions 11–20

Complete the notes below.

*Write **NO MORE THAN THREE WORDS** for each answer.*

Artist's Exhibition

General details:

Place: **11** .... No. 1 **12** ....

Dates: 6th October – **13** ....

Display details:

• jewellery

• furniture

• ceramics

• **14** ....

• sculpture

Expect to see: crockery in the shape of **15** ....

silver jewellery, e.g. large rings containing **16** ....

a shoe sculpture made out of **17** ....

Go to demonstrations called: **18** '.............................'

Artist's Conservatory

Courses include: Chinese brush painting

19 ....

silk painting

Fees include: Studio use

Access to the shop

Supply of **20** ....

Questions 21–30

Tip Strip

- Look at the whole task to see how many different types of question there are. In this case there are three. Two of these question types are familiar to you already from earlier tests.

Questions 21–23

Complete the sentences below.

Write **NO MORE THAN THREE WORDS** *for each answer.*

According to Alison Sharp ...

21 Bear ancestors date back
.... years.

22 Scientists think bears were originally
in the same family as ....

23 The Cave Bear was not dangerous
because it ....

Tip Strip

- **Questions 24–28**: Here you have five questions and six possible answers to choose from each time, so you can use any of the answers more than once if necessary.

- Read the five questions down the side of the grid very carefully and underline the key words before you listen. Do not underline any word which appears in more than one question as this indicates that it is not a key word.

Questions 24–28

Complete the grid. Tick (✓) the relevant boxes in each column.

Bear species	Sloth Bear	Giant Panda	Polar Bear	Black Bear	Brown Bear	Sun Bear
24 Which is the most recent species?						
25 Which is the largest looking bear?						
26 Which is the smallest bear?						
27 Which bear eats plants?						
28 Which bear eats insects						

Questions 29–30

Circle *TWO* letters *A–F*.

Which **TWO** actions are mentioned to help bears survive?

A   breeding bears in captivity

B   encouraging a more humane attitude

C   keeping bears in national parks

D   enforcing international laws

E   buying the speaker's book

F   writing to the United Nations

Questions 31–40

Questions 31–36

Circle the correct letters A–C.

31 The speaker compares a solar eclipse today to a

    A religious experience.

    B scientific event.

    C popular spectacle.

32 The speaker says that the dark spot of an eclipse is

    A simple to predict.

    B easy to explain.

    C randomly occurring.

33 Concerning an eclipse, the ancient Chinese were

    A fascinated.

    B rational.

    C terrified.

34 For the speaker, the most impressive aspect of an eclipse is the

    A exceptional beauty of the sky.

    B chance for scientific study.

    C effect of the moon on the sun.

35 Eclipses occur rarely because of the size of the

    A moon.

    B sun.

    C earth.

36 In predicting eclipses, the Babylonians were restricted by their

    A religious attitudes.

    B inaccurate observations.

    C limited ability to calculate.

Questions 37–40

Complete the table below.

Write **NO MORE THAN THREE WORDS** *for each answer.*

Date of eclipse	Scientists	Observation
1715	Halley	**37** .... who accurately predicted an eclipse
1868	Janssen and Lockyer	discovered **38** ....
1878	Watson	believed he had found **39** ....
1919	Einstein	realised astronomers had misunderstood **40** ....

Twist in the Tale

Fears that television and computers would kill children's desire to read couldn't have been more wrong. With sales roaring, a new generation of authors are publishing's newest and unlikeliest literary stars

A   Less than three years ago, doom merchants were predicting that the growth in video games and the rise of the Internet would sound the death knell for children's literature. But contrary to popular myth, children are reading more books than ever. A recent survey by Books Marketing found that children up to the age of 11 read on average for four hours a week, particularly girls.

B   Moreover, the children's book market, which traditionally was seen as a poor cousin to the more lucrative and successful adult market, has come into its own. Publishing houses are now making considerable profits on the back of new children's books and children's authors can now command significant advances. 'Children's books are going through an incredibly fertile period,' says Wendy Cooling, a children's literature consultant. 'There's a real buzz around them. Book clubs are happening, sales are good, and people are much more willing to listen to children's authors.'

C   The main growth area has been the market for eight to fourteen-year-olds, and there is little doubt that the boom has been fuelled by the bespectacled apprentice, *Harry Potter*. So influential has J. K. Rowling's series of books been that they have helped to make reading fashionable for pre-teens. 'Harry made it OK to be seen on a bus reading a book,' says Cooling. 'To a child, that is important.' The current buzz around the publication of the fourth Harry Potter beats anything in the world of adult literature.

D   'People still tell me, "Children don't read nowadays",' says David Almond, the award-winning author of children's books such as *Skellig*. 'The truth is that they are skilled, creative readers. When I do classroom visits, they ask me very sophisticated questions about use of language, story structure, chapters and dialogue.' No one is denying that books are competing with other forms of entertainment for children's attention but it seems as though children find a special kind of mental nourishment within the printed page.

E   'A few years ago, publishers lost confidence and wanted to make books more like television, the medium that frightened them most,' says children's book critic Julia Eccleshare. 'But books aren't TV, and you will find that children always say that the good thing about books is that you can see them in your head. Children are demanding readers,' she says. 'If they don't get it in two pages, they'll drop it.'

F No more are children's authors considered mere sentimentalists or failed adult writers. 'Some feted adult writers would kill for the sales,' says Almond, who sold 42,392 copies of *Skellig* in 1999 alone. And advances seem to be growing too: UK publishing outfit Orion recently negotiated a six-figure sum from US company Scholastic for *The Seeing Stone,* a children's novel by Kevin Crossley-Holland, the majority of which will go to the author.

G It helps that once smitten, children are loyal and even fanatical consumers. Author Jacqueline Wilson says that children spread news of her books like a bushfire. 'My average reader is a girl of ten,' she explains. 'They're sociable and acquisitive. They collect. They have parties – where books are a good present. If they like something, they have to pass it on.' After Rowling, Wilson is currently the best-selling children's writer, and her sales have boomed over the past three years. She has sold more than three million books, but remains virtually invisible to adults, although most ten-year-old girls know about her.

H Children's books are surprisingly relevant to contemporary life. Provided they are handled with care, few topics are considered off-limits for children. One senses that children's writers relish the chance to discuss the whole area of topics and language. But Anne Fine, author of many award-winning children's books is concerned that the British literati still ignore children's culture. 'It's considered worthy but boring,' she says.

I 'I think there's still a way to go,' says Almond, who wishes that children's books were taken more seriously as literature. Nonetheless, he derives great satisfaction from his child readers. 'They have a powerful literary culture,' he says. 'It feels as if you're able to step into the store of mythology and ancient stories that run through all societies and encounter the great themes: love and loss and death and redemption.'

J At the moment, the race is on to find the next Harry Potter. The bidding for new books at Bologna this year – the children's equivalent of the Frankfurt Book Fair – was as fierce as anything anyone has ever seen. All of which bodes well for the long-term future of the market – and for children's authors, who have traditionally suffered the lowest profile in literature, despite the responsibility of their role.

Questions 1–7

*Look at the following list of people **A–E** and the list of statements (Questions 1–7).*
Match each statement with one of the people listed.

*Write the appropriate letters **A–E** in boxes 1–7 on your answer sheet.*

1   Children take pleasure in giving books to each other.

2   Reading in public is an activity that children have not
     always felt comfortable about doing.

3   Some well-known writers of adult literature regret that
     they earn less than popular children's writers.

4   Children are quick to decide whether they like or dislike
     a book.

5   Children will read many books by an author that they
     like.

6   The public do not realise how much children read today.

7   We are experiencing a rise in the popularity of
     children's literature.

A	Wendy Cooling
B	David Almond
C	Julia Eccleshare
D	Jacqueline Wilson
E	Anne Fine

Questions 8–10

*Using **NO MORE THAN THREE WORDS** taken from the reading passage, answer the*
following questions.

Write your answers in boxes 8–10 on your answer sheet.

8   For which age group have sales of books risen the most?

9   Which company has just invested heavily in an unpublished children's book?

10   Who is currently the best-selling children's writer?

Questions 11–14

*Reading Passage 1 has ten paragraphs **A–J**.*

Which paragraph mentions the following (Questions 11–14)?

*Write the appropriate letters (**A–J**) in boxes 11–14 on your answer sheet.*

11   the fact that children are able to identify and discuss the important
     elements of fiction

12   the undervaluing of children's society

13   the impact of a particular fictional character on the sales of children's books

14   an inaccurate forecast regarding the reading habits of children

You should spend about 20 minutes on **Questions 15–27**, which are based on Reading Passage 2 below.

Questions 15–21

Reading Passage 2 has nine paragraphs **A–I**.

From the list of headings below choose the most suitable heading for each paragraph.

Write the appropriate numbers (**i–xi**) in boxes 15–21 on your answer sheet.

List of headings

i Wide differences in leisure activities according to income

ii Possible inconsistencies in Ms Costa's data

iii More personal income and time influence leisure activities

iv Investigating the lifestyle problem from a new angle

v Increased incomes fail to benefit everyone

vi A controversial development offers cheaper leisure activities

vii Technology heightens differences in living standards

viii The gap between income and leisure spending closes

ix Two factors have led to a broader range of options for all

x Have people's lifestyles improved?

xi High earners spend less on leisure

Example	Answer
Paragraph E	iii

15 Paragraph A

16 Paragraph B

17 Paragraph C

18 Paragraph D

19 Paragraph F

20 Paragraph G

21 Paragraph H

Fun for the Masses

Americans worry that the distribution of income is increasingly unequal. Examining leisure spending changes that picture.

A Are you better off than you used to be? Even after six years of sustained economic growth, Americans worry about that question. Economists who plumb government income statistics agree that Americans' incomes, as measured in inflation-adjusted dollars, have risen more slowly in the past two decades than in earlier times, and that some workers' real incomes have actually fallen. They also agree that by almost any measure, income is distributed less equally than it used to be. Neither of those claims, however, sheds much light on whether living standards are rising or falling. This is because 'living standard' is a highly amorphous concept. Measuring how much people earn is relatively easy, at least compared with measuring how well they live.

B A recent paper by Dora Costa, an economist at the Massachusetts Institute of Technology, looks at the living-standards debate from an unusual direction. Rather than worrying about cash incomes, Ms Costa investigates Americans' recreational habits over the past century. She finds that people of all income levels have steadily increased the amount of time and money they devote to having fun. The distribution of dollar incomes may have become more skewed in recent years, but leisure is more evenly spread than ever.

C Ms Costa bases her research on consumption surveys dating back as far as 1888. The industrial workers surveyed in that year spent, on average, three-quarters of their incomes on food, shelter and clothing. Less than 2% of the average family's income was spent on leisure but that average hid large disparities. The share of a family's budget that was spent on having fun rose sharply with its income: the lowest-income families in this working-class sample spent barely 1% of their budgets on recreation, while higher earners spent more than 3%. Only the latter group could afford such extravagances as theatre and concert

performances, which were relatively much more expensive than they are today.

D Since those days, leisure has steadily become less of a luxury. By 1991, the average household needed to devote only 38% of its income to the basic necessities, and was able to spend 6% on recreation. Moreover, Ms Costa finds that the share of the family budget spent on leisure now rises much less sharply with income than it used to. At the beginning of this century a family's recreational spending tended to rise by 20% for every 10% rise in income. By 1972–73, a 10% income gain led to roughly a 15% rise in recreational spending, and the increase fell to only 13% in 1991. What this implies is that Americans of all income levels are now able to spend much more of their money on having fun.

E One obvious cause is that real income overall has risen. If Americans in general are richer, their consumption of entertainment goods is less likely to be affected by changes in their income. But Ms Costa reckons that rising incomes are responsible for, at most, half of the changing structure of leisure spending. Much of the rest may be due to the fact that poorer Americans have more time off than they used to. In earlier years, low-wage workers faced extremely long hours and enjoyed few days off. But since the 1940s, the less skilled (and lower paid) have worked ever-fewer hours, giving them more time to enjoy leisure pursuits.

F Conveniently, Americans have had an increasing number of recreational possibilities to choose from. Public investment in sports complexes, parks and golf courses has made leisure cheaper and more accessible. So too has technological innovation. Where listening to music used to imply paying for concert tickets or owning a piano, the invention of the radio made music accessible to everyone and virtually free. Compact discs, videos and other paraphernalia have widened the choice even further.

G At a time when many economists are pointing accusing fingers at technology for causing a widening inequality in the wages of skilled and unskilled workers, Ms Costa's research gives it a much more egalitarian face. High earners have always been able to afford amusement. By lowering the price of entertainment, technology has improved the standard of living of those in the lower end of the income distribution. The implication of her results is that once recreation is taken into account, the differences in Americans' living standards may not have widened so much after all.

H These findings are not water-tight. Ms Costa's results depend heavily upon what exactly is classed as a recreational expenditure. Reading is an example. This was the most popular leisure activity for working men in 1888, accounting for one-quarter of all recreational spending. In 1991, reading took only 16% of the entertainment dollar. But the American Department of Labour's expenditure surveys do not distinguish between the purchase of a mathematics tome and that of a best-selling novel. Both are classified as recreational expenses. If more money is being spent on textbooks and professional books now than in earlier years, this could make 'recreational' spending appear stronger than it really is.

I Although Ms Costa tries to address this problem by showing that her results still hold even when tricky categories, such as books, are removed from the sample, the difficulty is not entirely eliminated. Nonetheless, her broad conclusion seems fair. Recreation is more available to all and less dependent on income. On this measure at least, inequality of living standards has fallen.

Questions 22–26

Complete each of the following statements (Questions 22–26) using words from the box.

*Write the appropriate letter **A–H** in boxes 22–26 on your answer sheet.*

22 It is easier to determine ……. than living standards.

23 A decrease in ……… during the 20th century led to a bigger investment in leisure.

24 According to Ms Costa, how much Americans spend on leisure has been directly affected by salaries and ……… .

25 The writer notes both positive and negative influences of ……… .

26 According to the writer, the way Ms Costa defined ……… may have been misleading.

A	recreational activities
B	the family budget
C	holiday time
D	government expenditure
E	computer technology
F	income levels
G	non-luxury spending
H	professional reading
I	high-income earners

Question 27

*Choose the appropriate letter **A–D** and write it in box 27 on your answer sheet.*

The writer thinks that Ms Costa

A provides strong evidence to support her theory.

B displays serious flaws in her research methods.

C attempts to answer too many questions.

D has a useful overall point to make.

THE ART OF HEALING

As with so much, the medicine of the Tang dynasty left its European counterpart in the shade. It boasted its own 'national health service', and left behind the teachings of the incomparable Sun Simiao

If no further evidence was available of the sophistication of China in the Tang era, then a look at Chinese medicine would be sufficient. At the Western end of the Eurasian continent the Roman empire had vanished, and there was nowhere new to claim the status of the cultural and political centre of the world. In fact, for a few centuries, this centre happened to be the capital of the Tang empire, and Chinese medicine under the Tang was far ahead of its European counterpart. The organisational context of health and healing was structured to a degree that had no precedence in Chinese history and found no parallel elsewhere.

An Imperial Medical Office had been inherited from previous dynasties: it was immediately restructured and staffed with directors and deputy directors, chief and assistant medical directors, pharmacists and curators of medicinal herb gardens and further personnel. Within the first two decades after consolidating its rule, the Tang administration set up one central and several provincial medical colleges with professors, lecturers, clinical practitioners and pharmacists to train students in one or all of the four departments of medicine, acupuncture, physical therapy and exorcism.

Physicians were given positions in governmental medical service only after passing qualifying examinations. They were remunerated in accordance with the number of cures they had effected during the past year.

In 723 Emperor Xuanzong personally composed a general formulary of prescriptions recommended to him by one of his imperial pharmacists and sent it to all the provincial medical schools. An Arabic traveller, who visited China in 851, noted with surprise that prescriptions from the emperor's formulary were publicised on notice boards at crossroads to enhance the welfare of the population.

The government took care to protect the general populace from potentially harmful medical practice. The Tang legal code was the first in China to include laws concerned with harmful and heterodox medical practices. For example, to treat patients for money without adhering to standard procedures was defined as fraud combined with theft and had to be tried in accordance with the legal statutes on theft. If such therapies resulted in the death of a patient, the healer was to be banished for two and a half years. In case a physician purposely failed to practice according to the standards, he was to be tried in accordance with the statutes on premeditated homicide. Even if no harm resulted, he was to be sentenced to sixty strokes with a heavy cane.

In fact, physicians practising during the Tang era had access to a wealth of pharmaceutical and medical texts, their contents ranging from purely pragmatic advice to highly sophisticated theoretical considerations. Concise descriptions of the position, morphology, and functions of the organs of the human body stood side by side in libraries with books enabling readers to calculate the daily, seasonal and annual climatic conditions of cycles of sixty years and to understand and predict their effects on health.

Several Tang authors wrote large collections of prescriptions, continuing a literary tradition documented since the 2nd century BC. The two most outstanding works to be named here were those by Sun Simiao (581–682?) and Wang Tao (c.670–755). The latter was a librarian who copied more than six thousand formulas, categorised in 1,104 sections, from sixty-five older works and published them under the title *Waitai miyao*. Twenty-four sections, for example, were devoted to ophthalmology. They reflect the Indian origin of much Chinese knowledge on ailments of the eye and, in particular, of cataract surgery.

Sun Simiao was the most eminent physician and author not only of the Tang dynasty, but of the entire first millennium AD. He was a broadly educated intellectual and physician; his world view integrated notions of all three of the major currents competing at his time – Confucianism, Daoism and Buddhism. Sun Simiao gained fame during his lifetime as a clinician (he was summoned to the imperial court at least once) and as author of the *Prescriptions Worth Thousands in Gold (Qianjinfang)* and its sequel. In contrast to developments in the 12th century, physicians relied on prescriptions and single substances to treat their patients' illnesses. The theories of systematic correspondences, characteristic of the acupuncture tradition, had not been extended to cover pharmacology yet.

Sun Simiao rose to the pantheon of Chinese popular Buddhism in about the 13th century. He was revered as paramount Medicine God. He gained this extraordinary position in Chinese collective memory not only because he was an outstanding clinician and writer, but also for his ethical concerns. Sun Simiao was the first Chinese author known to compose an elaborate medical ethical code. Even though based on Buddhist and Confucian values, his deontology is comparable to the Hippocratic Oath. It initiated a debate on the task of medicine, its professional obligations, social position and moral justification that continued until the arrival of Western medicine in the 19th century.

Despite or – more likely – because of its long-lasting affluence and political stability, the Tang dynasty did not add any significantly new ideas to the interpretation of illness, health and healing. Medical thought reflects human anxieties; changes in medical thought always occur in the context of new existential fears or of fundamentally changed social circumstances. Nevertheless, medicine was a most fascinating ingredient of Tang civilisation and it left a rich legacy to subsequent centuries.

Questions 28–30

*Choose the appropriate letters **A–D** and write them in boxes 28–30 on your answer sheet.*

28 In the first paragraph, the writer draws particular attention to
   A the lack of medical knowledge in China prior to the Tang era.
   B the Western interest in Chinese medicine during the Tang era.
   C the systematic approach taken to medical issues during the Tang era.
   D the rivalry between Chinese and Western cultures during the Tang era.

29 During the Tang era, a government doctor's annual salary depended upon
   A the effectiveness of his treatment.
   B the extent of his medical experience.
   C the number of people he had successfully trained.
   D the breadth of his medical expertise.

30 Which of the following contravened the law during the Tang era?
   A a qualified doctor's refusal to practise
   B the use of unorthodox medical practices
   C a patient dying under medical treatment
   D the receipt of money for medical treatment

Questions 31–37

Do the following statements agree with the information given in Reading Passage 3?

In boxes 31–37 on your answer sheet write

YES   *if the statement agrees with the information*
NO   *if the statement contradicts the information*
NOT GIVEN   *if there is no information on this in the passage*

31 Academic staff sometimes taught a range of medical subjects during the Tang era.
32 The medical knowledge available during the Tang era only benefited the wealthy.
33 Tang citizens were encouraged to lead a healthy lifestyle.
34 Doctors who behaved in a fraudulent manner were treated in the same way as ordinary criminals during the Tang era.
35 Medical reference books published during the Tang era covered practical and academic issues.
36 *Waitai miyao* contained medical data from the Tang era.
37 Chinese medical authors are known to have influenced Indian writing.

Questions 38–40

Complete the sentences below with words taken from Reading Passage 3.

*Use **NO MORE THAN THREE WORDS** for each answer.*

Write your answers in boxes 38–40 on your answer sheet.

The first known medical writing in China dates back to the … **38** … .

During the Tang era, doctors depended most on … **39** … and … to treat their patients.

… **40** … is famous for producing a set of medical rules for Chinese physicians.

Writing module (1 hour)

You should spend about 20 minutes on this task.

> *The graph and pie chart below give information on in-house training courses in a large financial company.*
>
> *Write a report for a university lecturer describing the information shown below.*

You should write at least 150 words.

Training – hours per year

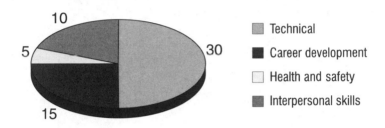

- ■ Technical
- ■ Career development
- □ Health and safety
- ■ Interpersonal skills

Office Workers' Attitude to Training

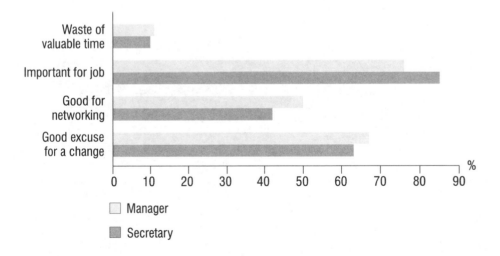

You should spend about 40 minutes on this task.

Present a written argument or case to an educated non-specialist audience on the following topic:

> *To be labelled a 'Work of Art', a painting, sculpture or other art form should display certain qualities that are unique. However, over the past century there has been a decline in the quality of prize-winning artwork and it is now possible for quite ordinary pieces of art to be labelled 'masterpieces' whilst true works of art pass unnoticed.*
>
> *Do you agree or disagree? Give reasons for your answer.*

You should write at least 250 words.

You should use your own ideas, knowledge and experience and support your arguments with examples and relevant evidence.

Speaking module (11–14 minutes)

PART 1

The examiner will ask you some questions about yourself, such as:

¥ *What part of your country do you come from?*

¥ *How long have you lived there?*

¥ *How do you like to travel around?*

¥ *What type of restaurants are there in your city/town/village?*

¥ *Which is your favourite? Why?*

¥ *What sort of food do your parents like to eat?*

PART 2 The topic for your talk will be written on a card which the examiner will hand you. Read it carefully and then make some brief notes.

Your school days

INSTRUCTIONS
Please read the topic below carefully. You will be asked to talk about it for 1 to 2 minutes.

You have one minute to think about what you re going to say.
You can make some notes to help you if you wish.

Describe an enjoyable event that you experienced when you were at school.

You should say: when it happened
                     what was good about it
                     why you particularly remember this event

---

At the end of your talk, the examiner will ask one or two brief questions to signal that it time to stop talking. For example, he or she might say:

Did you enjoy your time at school?
Would you recommend your school to others?

PART 3 Once your talk in Part 2 is over, your examiner will ask you further questions related to the topic in Part 2. The examiner may ask you to speak about these points.

School

¥ *single sex - vs - co-educational schools*

¥ *school uniforms*

¥ *the teacher as authority or friend*

¥ *the role of the teacher in the language classroom*

¥ *education - vs - training*

GENERAL TRAINING MODULE

Reading (1 hour)

PART 1

*You are advised to spend 20 minutes on **Questions 1–14**.*

Look at the article on page 131 about holidays and at the statements (1–8) below.

Questions 1–8

In boxes 1–8 on your answer sheet write

TRUE *if the statement is true*
FALSE *if the statement is false*
NOT GIVEN *if the information is not given in the passage*

1 Solving problems can be hard work for the holiday-maker.

2 The most common problem for holiday-makers is crowded airports.

3 Overall, holiday accommodation poses few problems.

4 Tour companies provide a satisfactory level of information to holiday-makers.

5 A low-cost holiday should still offer some high-quality services.

6 Hotel staff can advise you on who you should complain to.

7 Photographs may help to support an argument about a holiday problem.

8 If you are not good at writing letters, find someone to help you.

Having a Lovely Time?

A chance to relax and leave your worries behind? For some, holidays are nothing but trouble as the results of one survey showed

When you think about it, it's amazing that anyone gets away with a carefree holiday. It seems there is limitless potential for things to go wrong, from flight delays and lost luggage to poor accommodation.

A recent questionnaire showed that a third of people who replied had a complaint about their holiday last year. And when these unhappy holiday-makers discussed the problem with their tour company nearly half said it involved time and effort on their part to resolve things.

When asked exactly what the reasons were for their dissatisfaction top of the list was flight delays and 20 per cent of holiday-makers to Europe said they had to wait up to an hour.

More worrying is the fact that almost a third of holiday-makers who had complained said it was about the apartment or hotel room they had been allocated. There is an enormous variety of holiday accommodation and we recommend that consumers look for places that have been inspected by the Tourist Boards; this way they can have the confidence that they will get the type of accommodation they are looking for. It seems that tour companies now offer more honest accurate brochures though. Eight-five per cent of holiday-makers who responded to our questionnaire said the description offered by the company matched the place they visited and the facilities provided.

This is good news for the industry and for holiday-makers. A holiday is a major purchase – yet it's one we can't try before we pay. All we have to go on is the brochure and it's a credit to tour operators that they now contain more detail.

OUR ADVICE

DO be realistic. No one should be palmed off with a poor standard of service, food or accommodation even if you paid a rock-bottom price for a last-minute break. However, be reasonable – you won't get a room with the best view in town if you've paid a budget price.

DO complain to the right person. Moaning to the waiter about a week's worth of appalling food, then writing an indignant letter when you get back home won't have the same impact as airing your grievances at the time.

DO get evidence for a serious problem such as having a building site instead of the promised swimming pool below your window. Take a photo to back up your case.

DON'T write and complain for the sake of it. Letters can be powerful as long as they're about something you have a good reason to complain about.

DON'T lose your temper. Easier said than done, but you're more likely to get results if you state your case firmly, explain why you think there's a problem then suggest a reasonable solution.

Now read the information on page 133 and answer Questions 9–14.

Questions 9–14

Match the car-hire websites on page 133 to the statements 9–14.

Write the appropriate letters (A–H) in boxes 9–14 on your answer sheet.

NB Some of the websites may be chosen more than once.

Example	*Answer*
The company assures customers that their car hire is the cheapest.	D

9   It is possible to see what the cars look like.

10   Assistance is provided with some holiday routes.

11   You will get cheaper car hire if you have used the company before.

12   Attempts made by the writer to book a car were unsuccessful.

13   You can only hire a car in certain locations.

14   The site is suited to people with up-to-date hardware.

Hiring a Car Online

Online car hire promises to be cheap, quick and convenient.
But is it? Neil McDougall revs up his mouse

A Autos.com

Just click on the reservations button, fill in your home country, destination and dates, pick a car and you're into the booking form without any fuss and with all the charges, fixed and optional, laid out. There's also a detailed rental guide explaining your contract.

B Cash.com.uk

One to consider if you're going to the States, although, after I'd worked through half the booking process, it returned an error message without telling me which element of the procedure needed adjusting. I got there in the end. There is an inspirational section with detailed directions for some of the great drives of America.

C Expeed.org.uk

Book a flight with Expeed and when you continue on to the car-hire section, the software already knows where you are going and when. However, you seem to be restricted to cities with airports for your car hire, and additional taxes are presented in travel-agent speak.

D Cutprice.com

Is currently offering an aggressive lowest rates guarantee, an extra discount for former Holtravel clients and a package of free gifts to sweeten the deal. It also commits to no insurance excess on any of their rentals anywhere.

E Hot.org

Straightforward to navigate, with plenty of information on rental requirements and rules of operation. There are photographs of the types of vehicles available, leaving no doubt what a 'premium' or 'compact' car is. It took me just seconds to start reserving a car but then the whole thing ground to a halt and refused all attempts to access the reservation system.

F Cars.net

Another site offering discounts for booking online, but also special late deals (for example £35 off a Renault Megane in Majorca last week). Prices are fully inclusive of insurance and there is a reassuringly large small-print section.

G Cover.org

A three-step process to rent cars in 70 countries. Very flash and slick, so much so that people with older computers may have trouble getting this information. Limited selection of online tourist attractions (but that's more than most give you). Graphically complex but impressive booking system.

H Cheapandcheerful.net.uk

Avoids unnecessary embellishments online but the booking procedure is as good as it gets. Enter how many miles you expect to drive and tick your insurance, driver and child-seat choices and they will all be included in the final price. You must contact the location directly if you need a car within 3 days. And to hire a car abroad, there's a dull email form to fill in and they'll get back to you.

You are advised to spend 20 minutes on **Questions 15–26**. Look at the book extract on page 135.

Questions 15–20

From the list of headings below choose the most suitable heading for each paragraph A–G.

Write the appropriate numbers (**i–x**) in boxes 15–20 on your answer sheet.

List of headings

i	Gathering source material
ii	Open-ended essays
iii	The importance of focusing on the task
iv	Writing the essay
v	Types of essay and their purpose
vi	Learning from the essay
vii	Making the support material relevant
viii	Reviewing and amending the essay
ix	Allocating your personal resources
x	Writing a framework

---

15 Paragraph A

Example	Answer
Paragraph B	ix

16 Paragraph C

17 Paragraph D

18 Paragraph E

19 Paragraph F

20 Paragraph G

STUDY NOTES SERIES
Chapter Seven
ESSAY WRITING

A Essays, whether written as part of a secondary school programme or further education course, are designed to test your thinking, writing and study skills. Creative essays offer you the freedom to demonstrate your abilities to communicate effectively. Analytical essays, on the other hand, will require you to show that you have researched the topic and drawn on the work of others to come to your conclusion.

B The amount of time and effort you devote to writing an essay will depend on how it fits into the overall scheme of assessment and should be in direct proportion to the percentage of marks allotted. If the essay constitutes part of your coursework, the time and effort required will depend on what marks, if any, are going towards your overall mark and grade.

C However interesting and well prepared your essay may be, if it does not address the question, you will not receive a good mark. It is therefore essential that you examine the question and understand what is required. A list of key words which may appear in an essay question is provided in Appendix 4. Be sure you know what is being asked for and then consider what information is relevant and what is not.

D Use a variety of relevant background texts, refer to your lecture notes and heed any advice given by your lecturer. When you collect material, always ask yourself what questions need to be answered and then take good notes in your own words. Begin notes on each source on a new page and do not forget to record details of the author, title of the book and date of publication. Remember that copying words from another writer's work without acknowledging the source constitutes the serious crime of plagiarism.

E Once you have collected your source material you should then sketch out a plan. Begin by writing three or four sentences, which provide a summary of the essay. You can amend or add to the plan as you proceed and it provides a useful scaffold for your essay. It also ensures that you cover all the main themes and that your essay focuses on the question. Ideally you should plan to examine the question from all sides, presenting various views before reaching a conclusion based on the evidence.

F The introduction to the essay should explain to the reader how you are going to tackle the question and provide an outline of what will follow. Then move on to the main body of the essay. Refer to your notes and develop two or three logical arguments. Begin each paragraph with a topic sentence, which clearly states the subject to be discussed, and then use the remainder of the paragraph to fill out this opening sentence. A good essay should finish rather than simply stop. That is to say, the conclusion should provide a statement of your final position, summing up the arguments that your opinions are based upon.

G It is important to keep the essay relevant and to provide some examples, quotations, illustrations, diagrams or maps wherever appropriate. However, it is equally important to avoid the temptation to pad your essay with unwanted information: this wastes your time and undermines the relevant parts of the essay. In coursework and assessment essays not written under examination conditions, do not forget to acknowledge your sources in a bibliography.

*Now read the information below and answer **Questions 21–26** pn page 137.*

School of Design
COURSE GUIDELINES

2.1 Assignments

Coursework assignments will involve the production of an artefact (something shaped by human beings rather than by nature) OR an investigation of some kind followed by a report. This is to demonstrate the relevance of your study to society today. If you opt to produce an artefact, (e.g. a working model or piece of machinery) you will also be expected to provide some written explanation of how and why you produced it.

You need to follow these steps:

• Find out precisely what is expected of you. Talk to your tutor and refer to the syllabus document.

• Be aware of what skills and abilities you must demonstrate.

• Always plan a project thoroughly before you begin it but be realistic about how much time you can seriously devote to it.

Choosing a topic

Remember that this course is essentially concerned with the achievement of desired ends. So first identify a real-life problem, then consider it in detail, specify a precise need and then define your design task. As you plan, wherever possible, consider using new materials, techniques and technology such as computer-aided design (CAD).

There is nothing wrong with talking to knowledgeable people about your project; in fact, this shows initiative. However, the project is yours so you must do the work yourself.

You will need a fairly flexible plan because sometimes resources, apparatus and consumables may not be available when you need them. It is a good idea to work backwards when planning so you know you will meet your final deadline. Finally, when you plan the various stages of your project give due regard to safety and costs.

Questions 21–26

Look at the Course Guidelines for students on how to approach a design project.

*Complete the sentences below using **NO MORE THAN THREE WORDS** for each answer.*

Write your answers in boxes 21–26.

21   There are ………….. types of assignment to choose from.

22   A working model must be accompanied by ………………… of some sort.

23   In order to understand the purpose of the assignment, students are advised to read ………………………… .

24   Topics must be based on …………………… .

25   To avoid handing the assignment in late, it is suggested that students …………………… .

26   As well as being cost effective, the method chosen must also be …………………… .

*You should spend about 20 minutes on **Questions 27–40** which are based on the reading passage below.*

A Stone Age Approach to Exercise

Forget those long arduous sessions in the gym. If you want to stay fighting fit, try a modern Stone Age workout* instead

Art De Vany is 62, but physical fitness tests three years ago showed he had the body of a 32-year-old. Although De Vany is sceptical of such assessments, he knows he's in good shape. His former career as a professional baseball player may have something to do with it, but he attributes his physical prowess to an exercise regime inspired by the lifestyles of our Palaeolithic ancestors.

De Vany's advice to the modern exercise freak is to cut duration and frequency, and increase intensity. 'Our muscle fibre composition reveals that we are adapted to extreme intensity of effort,' says De Vany, a professor of economics at the Institute of Mathematical Behavioral Sciences at the University of California, Irvine. His approach to fitness combines Darwinian thinking with his interest in chaos theory and complex systems.

This new science, which De Vany calls evolutionary fitness, is part of growing efforts to understand how the human body has been shaped by evolution, and to use this knowledge to improve our health and fitness. Proponents believe the key lies in the lifestyle of our hunter-gatherer ancestors because, they say, the vast majority of the human genome is still adapted to an ancient rhythm of life which swung between intense periods of activity and long stretches of inertia.

Across the Palaeolithic age – which covers the period between 2.6 million and 10,000 years ago – prey animals were large, fast on their feet, or both. For men, this would have meant lots of walking or jogging to find herds, dramatic sprints, jumps and turns, perhaps violent struggles, and long walks home carrying the kill. Women may not have had such intense exercise, but they would have spent many hours walking to sources of water or food, digging up tubers, and carrying children. If modern hunter-gatherers are anything to go by, men may have hunted for up to four days a week and travelled 15 kilometres or more on each trip. Women may have gathered food every two or three days. There would also have been plenty of other regular physical activities for both sexes such as skinning animals and tool making, and probably dancing.

Our ancestors must have evolved cardiovascular, metabolic and thermoregulatory systems capable of sustaining high-level aerobic exertion under the hot African sun, according to Loren Cordain of the Human Performance Laboratory at Colorado State University. And given that the Palaeolithic era ended only an evolutionary blink of an eye ago, we ignore its legacy at our peril. Cordain and his colleagues point out that in today's developed societies, inactivity is associated with disease. Contemporary hunter-gatherer societies rarely experience these modern killers, they say.

This is where De Vany's exercise ideas come in. 'The primary objectives for any exercise and diet programme must be to counter hyper-insulinaemia (chronically elevated insulin) and hypoexertion (wasting of the body's lean mass through inactivity),' he writes in his forthcoming book about evolutionary exercise. Exercise and diet are linked. For example, says De Vany, our appetite control mechanisms work best when our activity mimics that of our ancestors. But he feels that most modern exercise regimes are not hitting the mark.

De Vany views the body as non-linear and dynamic and says exercise should mix order and chaos. 'Chronic aerobic exercise overstrains the heart, reducing the chaotic variation in the heart rate which is essential to health,' he says. Likewise, most weight training is governed too much by routine and is too time-consuming. He gives his own workout a chaotic character with ascending weights and descending repetitions. To these brief but intense gym workouts he adds a wide variety of other activities that vary randomly in intensity and duration. These include roller blading, bicycling, walking, sprinting, tennis, basketball, power walking, hitting softballs and trekking with a grandson on his shoulders.

He also argues that most people do not train the right muscles for that ultimately attractive – and adaptive – quality of symmetry. 'Symmetry is a reliable evolutionary clue to health,' he says. 'Tumours and pathologies produce gross asymmetries, and our love of symmetry reflects the reproductive success of our ancestors, who were sensitive to these clues.' He strives for the X-look – a symmetrical balance of mass in the shoulder girdle, upper chest and back, the calves and lower quads, two of the four large muscles at the front of the thighs. This also makes men look taller, he adds, 'another reliable evolutionary clue that women use to find good genes'.

The hunter-gatherer lifestyle indicates that women should exercise only a little less intensely than men, says De Vany. 'Women are opportunistic hunters who go after small game when they come across it. They also climb trees to capture honey and snare birds. And have you ever seen how much work it is to dig out a deep tuber?' Women benefit enormously from strength work, he says. It increases their bone density and they get and stay leaner by building muscle mass. 'Today's women are so weak [compared with their female ancestors].'

Of course, people vary. De Vany acknowledges that our ancestors were adapted to a variety of terrains and climates. Cordain points out that genetic differences between populations lead to different physical strengths. East Africans, for example, seem to be better endurance runners, West Africans better sprinters. But human genetic similarity greatly outweighs the variations. And because our genes have changed so very little since Palaeolithic times, if you want to be a lean, mean, survival machine why not try exercising like a caveman?

*Workout = physical exercise session.

Questions 27–28

*Choose the appropriate letters **A–D** and write them in boxes 27–28 on your answer sheet.*

27 What do you learn about Art De Vany in the first paragraph?

    A He frequently tests his health.

    B He works as a professional sports player.

    C He is older than he appears to be.

    D He believes he has inherited a strong body.

28 In the second paragraph, De Vany recommends that people should

    A exercise less frequently.

    B exercise harder but for less time.

    C give their muscles more time to recover from exercise.

    D learn more about how the human body reacts to exercise.

Questions 29–31

*Choose **THREE** letters **A–G** and write them in boxes 29–31 on your answer sheet.*

Which **THREE** of the following does the writer highlight when discussing the lifestyle of our Palaeolithic ancestors?

A the difficulties involved in finding food

B their size compared to that of modern man

C the sudden movements required during their daily activities

D the aggressive nature of their negotiations with others

E the fact that life was equally energetic for both sexes

F the predictable frequency of physical activity

G the long distances between neighbours' homes

Question 32

*Choose the appropriate letter **A–D** and write it in box 32 on your answer sheet.*

32 Cordain compares modern hunter-gatherer societies to Paleolithic societies in terms of their

    A ability to withstand high temperatures.

    B resistance to certain fatal illnesses.

    C healthy mix of work and leisure activities.

    D refusal to change their way of life.

Questions 33–36

Using NO MORE THAN THREE WORDS, *answer the following questions.*

Write your answers in boxes 33–36 on your answer sheet.

33 What term does De Vany use to describe his approach to physical exercise?

34 Which TWO opposing factors does De Vany say an exercise programme should include?

35 Which type of activity does de Vany criticise as being harmful?

36 Which type of exercise does De Vany practise on a regular basis?

Questions 37–40

Do the following statements agree with the information given in the reading passage?

In boxes 37–40 on your answer sheet write

TRUE   *if the statement is true*
FALSE   *if the statement is false*
NOT GIVEN *if the information is not given in the passage*

37 Our Palaeolithic ancestors were constantly active.

38 Female exercise programmes should vary according to the shape of the individual.

39 Geographical features have played a role in human physical development.

40 The importance of genetic differences in deciding on an exercise programme is minimal.

Writing module (1 hour)

You should spend about 20 minutes on this task.

> *You have just returned home after living with a family in an English–speaking country for six months. You now realise that you left a small bag of personal possessions in your room. Write to the family describing the things you left behind. Ask them to send some or all of them to you. Offer to cover the costs.*

You should write at least 150 words.

You do not need to write your own address.

Begin your letter as follows:

Dear

You should spend about 40 minutes on this task.

Present a written argument or case to an educated non-specialist audience on the following topic:

> *Popular hobbies and interests change over time and are more a reflection of trends and fashions than an indication of what individuals really want to do in their spare time.*
>
> *To what extent do you agree with this statement? Give reasons for your answer.*

You should write at least 250 words.

You should use your own ideas, knowledge and experience and support your arguments with examples and relevant evidence.

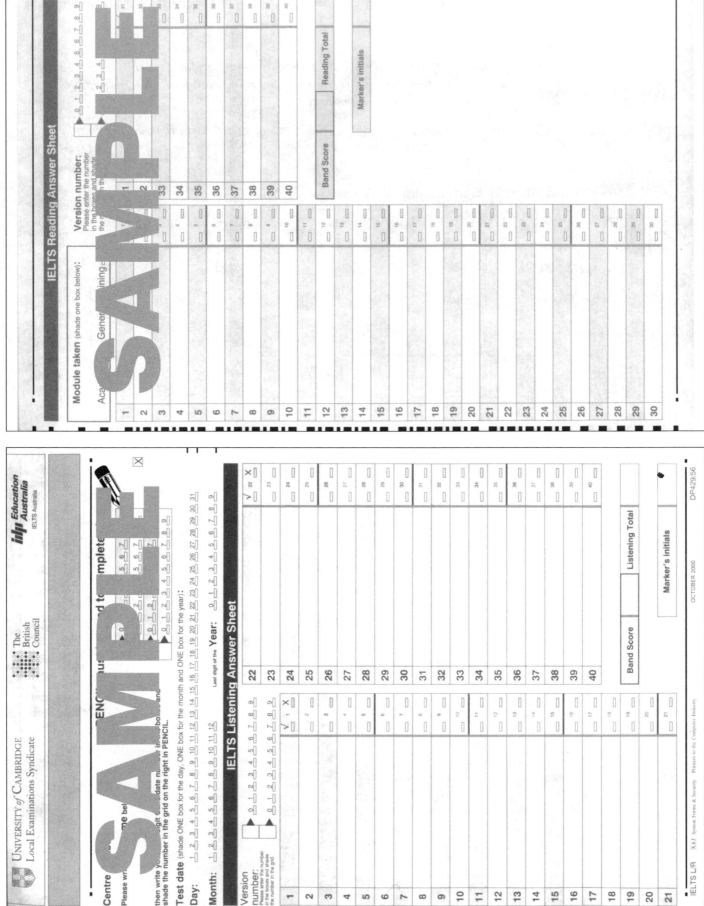

144

ANSWER KEY

Skills for IELTS

LISTENING

Exercise 1

1 the weather in your region/part of the world
2 which sport – results of a match
3 where/effects of the storm/possible dangers
4 which films/times of films/special deals

Exercise 2

a) 1 $25
    2 7.15pm
    3 C
b) 4 market research(er)/interviewer
    5 shampoo
    6 (a) free sample

Exercise 3

a) 2 How did the police arrive?
    3 What does the graph show?
    4 When was Louis Braille born?
b) 7 C (You heard 'four times a week', i.e. more than twice a week)
    8 A (You heard ' value for money', i.e. her choice is based on price)

Exercise 4

a) Main idea
    2 The way to succeed on the course.
    3 Different people have different interests.
    4 Describing coincidental meeting/surprise meeting
b) Supporting information
    2 hard work, hand assignments in on time, turn up for tutorials
    3 horses are their lives, I can't see the attraction
    4 It was Mike, all the way from Melbourne. What a coincidence!

Exercise 5

a) 9 spiders (main idea) mentioned three times
b) 10 B

Exercise 6

a) 11 1545
    12 more than 400
    13 raised/brought up
    14 (preserved) timbers
b) 15 C/G

Exercise 7

1 Opinion
2 Fact
3 Opinion
4 Fact

Exercise 8

16 Opinion: (The student <u>thinks</u> …)
    C
17 Opinion: (the <u>speaker's view</u>…)
    A

READING

Exercise 1

a) the title and sub-heading ✓
b) he introduction ✓
c) every part of the text
d) the first and last sentences of each paragraph in the main body ✓
e) the conclusion ✓
f) the middle of each paragraph

Exercise 2

a phone book – scan
a newspaper article you are interested in – skim
the film review page when looking for a film – scan
a letter from the bank – skim
a list of results for an exam you've taken – scan

Exercise 3

a) 1 B
    2 C
b) 1 para 5   3 para 4
    2 para 3   4 para 2

Exercise 5

Main idea: A
Topic sentence: When philosophers debate what it is that makes humans unique among animals, they often point to language.

Exercise 6

a) look for the topic sentences 3
b) select the right heading 4
c) read through the list of headings 1
d) skim the whole text 2

Exercise 7

a) Prices are stable. (Detail)
b) The economy is booming. (Main idea)
c) Consumer confidence is up. (Detail)
d) Interest rates are low. (Detail)

Exercise 8

a) a) predict the missing words 5
   b) read through the summary 1
   c) elect the best word for each gap 6
   d) skim the passage in order to locate the area being tested in the summary 3
   e) read around each gap in the summary 4
   f) check the instructions 2

b) 1 electricity/electric charge/current
   2 rain(drops)
   3 freezing

Exercise 9

a) select the questions that have key words that are easy to scan for 4
b) read the whole passage quickly 1
c) attempt the more difficult questions 6
d) skim the passage for an idea that is similar to the idea presented in the question 5
e) note any key words or main ideas within the paragraphs 2
f) read through the questions and underline the key words 3

Exercise 10

a) Computers have had a negative impact on children's reading habits. (Opinion)
b) Equatorial regions of the Earth have warm climates. (Fact)
c) Medical treatment has improved over the past century. (Fact)

Exercise 11

a) NO
b) NO
c) NOT GIVEN
d) YES

WRITING

Exercise 1

a 1 Tonnes of CO_2 emitted, per person, per year
  2 Organisation for Economic & Cultural Development
  3 The high level of CO_2 emissions in North America
  4 Low levels of CO_2 emissions in developing countries/high levels of CO_2 emissions in developed countries

b 1 The writer has started by describing what information the graph shows.
  2 Yes
  3 "North America is the chief culprit …'; 'Latin America and the Caribbean produce the smallest levels of CO_2 emission …'; 'European nations also emit huge amounts of CO_2 …'.
  4 The writer uses a variety of linking devices (e.g., 'also', however') and referents (e.g., 'this is almost double …').

Exercise 3

a The student believes that the Internet will have a negative effect upon formal education.
b 1 four
   2 first paragraph: indication of the writer's position
      last paragraph: re-statement of position
   3 to introduce the main idea in the paragraph

Exercise 4

Introduction: The Internet will have a negative effect on students' lives.
Body of the composition:
Paragraph 1
main ideas: The internet will reduce lecturer/student contact
supporting ideas: 'students do not need to spend so much time on campus'; 'the same may be true of lecturers'; 'in my home country tutors usually stress the importance of regular meetings'.
Paragraph 2
main ideas: Use of the Internet will damage students' health.
supporting ideas: 'Studying is … a very sedentary activity…'; 'going to campus offers a change of scenery, …
Conclusion: The Internet is a valuable source of information but it will have a negative effect upon education if we grow too dependent on it.

Exercise 6

Starting with A

1 The driving test was on Friday *so* I took the day off work.
2 The president was extremely unpopular *despite the fact that* the majority of people had voted for him.
3 The swimming team trained hard *but* went home unsuccessful.
4 Eat your dinner *and* go to bed.
5 I forgot to give my homework to the teacher *so* he/she didn't mark it.
6 I can't comment on the film *because* I haven't seen it.
7 People continue to smoke *and so* they continue to suffer from respiratory diseases.

Starting with B

1 I took Friday off work *because* of the driving test.
2 The majority of people voted for the president *despite the fact that/although* he was extremely unpopular.
3 The swimming team went home unsuccessful *despite the fact that/although* they had trained hard.
4 Go to bed *when* you have eaten your dinner.
5 My teacher didn't mark my homework *because* I forgot to give it to her.
6 I haven't seen the film *so* I can't comment on it.
7 People continue to suffer from respiratory diseases *because/as* they continue to smoke.

Exercise 7

The Australian government collects tax in a number of different ways. <u>Firstly</u> money is collected at source from everyone in Australia who has a job. <u>Income tax</u>, as this is known, can be as high as 48% for some people. <u>Secondly</u>, the government gains money by imposing a tax on all goods purchased or services received so that every time money changes hands a tax of 10% is paid. The term <u>services</u> includes anything from getting a haircut to having your house painted. <u>Another way</u> that the government raises money is by charging an additional tax on luxuries such as wine, tobacco or perfume. <u>In addition to this tax on luxuries</u>, there is a special tax on fuel which brings in a large amount of revenue for the government. Tax <u>on petrol</u> is also aimed at reducing the number of cars on the roads by discouraging motorists from using their cars.

Exercise 8

a This graph shows how, over a ten-year period, money was spent on different products in Asia, Europe and the United States. The products cited in the graph are computers, radios and telephones.

b Dear Sir/Madam,

I am writing to ask if you have found a bag which, I believe, I left on the train when I travelled to Dover. When I arrived home I realised that my bag was missing and so I am assuming that I left it on the train. Would you mind checking in your lost property office. It's a small, black bag with a handle on the top. Inside there are some personal possessions and my certificate which I received from the English course I attended.

SPEAKING

Exercise 2

1 But first I'll have to pass several general Chemistry exams. ✓
2 I am really looking forward to studying in this country. ✗
3 My mother is a chemical engineer and so I've always been interested in the field. ✓
4 I expect that life at university will be very different from life at school. ✗
5 I'm interested in working as an industrial chemist. ✓
6 I'm hoping to win a scholarship. ✗

Exercise 3

a • the person's appearance ✓
• their home
• reasons why you liked them ✓
• the name of the person ✓
• their hobbies ✓
• your relationship to the person ✓

Exercise 4

a 2 in my opinion
3 I'm convinced
4 I don't believe … I suppose
5 Personally, I believe
6 One of the best things about

Test 1

LISTENING

Section 1

1 C
2 C
3 D
4 McDonald/Macdonald/MacDonald
5 Post Office Box/PO Box 676
6 775431
7 credit card/Visa
8 D, F (any order)
9 A, F (any order)
10 after (the) exams

Section 2

11 473
12 (open) 2/two(-)seater
13 smooth
14 180 kilometres
15 frame (and) engine
16 instrument panel/instruments/stop-watch
17 30
18 light aircraft/plane
19 wings
20 rear wheels

Section 3

21 Out and About
22 (the) university/campus
23 B
24 C
25 B
26 A
27 ✗
28 South American
29 ✔
30 ✔✔

Section 4

31 human activity/activities
32 farming and drainage
33 Dirty Thirties/30s
34 dry thunderstorms
35 machine operators
36 drought
37 irrigation
38 two-thirds
39 salty/saline/toxic
40 crops/plants/agriculture

READING

Passage 1 In Praise of Amateurs

Answer	Location of answer in text
1 scientists	**Para 1**: ...*scientists were largely men of private means who pursued their interest in natural philosophy for their own edification. Only in the past century or two has it become possible to make a living from investigating the workings of nature.*
2 science	**Para 1**: *Today, science is an increasingly specialised and compartmentalised subject, the domain of experts ...*
3 fields	**Para 2**: *... amateurs are actively involved in such fields as acoustics ...*
4 co-operation/ collaboration	**Para 2**: *... some of whom rely heavily on their co-operation.* **Para 4**: *...a long tradition of collaboration between amateur and professional sky watchers.*
5 observations	**Para 4**: *This makes special kinds of observations possible.* The paragraph also refers to *valuable work observing* and *amateur observers.*
6 dinosaurs	**Para 5**: *... because of the near-universal interest in anything to do with dinosaurs.*
7 conservation programme	**Para 6**: *Over the past few years their observations have uncovered previously unknown trends and cycles ... prompting a habitat conservation programme.*
8 acknowledge	**Para 7**: *A more serious problem is the question of how professionals can best acknowledge ...*
9 B	Adrian Hunt calls it *recreational education.*
10 A	Dr. Fienberg jokes that they are *either locked up or have blown themselves to bits.*
11 D	Dr. Carlson criticises some professionals who *believe science should remain their exclusive preserve.*
12 B	Hunt says that *the best sensors for finding fossils are human eyes – lots of them.*
13 C	Rick Bonney discusses the different *terms* that have been used for amateur.

Passage 2 Reading the Screen

Answer	Location of answer in text
14 C	**Para 1**: *This second position is supported ... These studies argue that literacy can only be understood in its social and technical context.*
15 A	The first two sentences present the two contrasting views. The rest of the paragraph expands on these.
16 B	**Para 6**: *How should these new technologies ... . It isn't enough ... unless they are properly integrated ...* The rest of the paragraph supports option B as does the following paragraph.
17 D	A global view expressed in the final paragraph but particularly in first and last sentences.
18 YES	**Para 2**: *But the picture is not uniform and doesn't readily demonstrate the simple distinction between literate and illiterate which had been considered adequate since the middle of the 19th century.*
19 NO	**Para 3**: *While reading a certain amount of writing is as crucial as it has ever been in industrial societies, it is doubtful whether a fully extended grasp of either is as necessary as it was 30 or 40 years ago.*
20 NOT GIVEN	**Para 2**: Discusses the decline in *some aspects of reading and writing* and paragraph 4 looks at the importance of these skills but there is **no information** about a rise or fall in the number of people unable to read and write.
21 YES	**Para 4**: *On the other hand, it is also the case that ever-increasing numbers of people make their living out of writing, which is better rewarded than ever before.*
22 YES	**Para 4**: *While you may not need to read and write to watch television, you certainly need to be able to read and write in order to make programmes.*
23 NO	**Para 5**: *The computer has re-established a central place for the written word on the screen, which used to be entirely devoted to the image. There is even anecdotal evidence that children are mastering reading and writing in order to get on to the Internet.*

ANSWER KEY

24 manuscript	**Para 1**: … there was a distinction between those who could read print and those who could manage the more difficult task of reading manuscript.
25 (tabloid) newspapers	See the first sentence of paragraph 2.
26 shopping lists	**Para 3**: … research suggests that for many people the only use for writing, outside formal education, is the compilation of shopping lists.

Passage 3 The Revolutionary Bridges of Robert Maillart

Answer	Location of answer in text
27 x	The invention of the automobile created an irresistible demand for … vehicular bridges … The type of bridge needed for cars and trucks, however, is fundamentally different …
28 viii	… Maillart developed a unique method for designing bridges …
29 v	His crucial innovation was incorporating the bridge's arch and roadway into a form called the hollow-box arch, which would substantially reduce the bridge's expense by minimising the amount of concrete needed.
30 iii	His first masterpiece … gained little favourable publicity … on the contrary …
31 vii	His most important breakthrough … but the leading authorities of Swiss engineering would argue against his methods for the next quarter of a century.
32 ii	In 1991 it became the first concrete bridge to be designated an international historic landmark.
33 i	Maillart's hollow-box arch became the dominant design form … In Switzerland, professors finally began to teach Maillart's ideas, which then influenced a new generation of designers.
34 columns	**Para C**: In a conventional arch bridge the weight of the roadway is transferred by columns to the arch …
35 vertical walls	**Para C**: In Maillart's design, though, the roadway and arch were connected by three vertical walls …
36 hollow boxes	**Para C**: forming two hollow boxes running under the roadway …
37 D	**Para C**: … a form called the hollow-box arch, which would substantially reduce the bridge's expense by minimising the amount of concrete needed.
38 C	**Para D**: Maillart, who had founded his own construction firm in 1902, was unable to win any more bridge projects …
39 G	**Para E**: For aesthetic reasons, Maillart wanted a thinner arch and his solution was to connect the arch to the roadway with transverse walls.
40 F	**Para F**: Salginatobel … had the most dramatic setting of all his structures, vaulting 80 metres above the ravine of the Salgina brook.

Test 2

LISTENING

Section 1

1 B
2 A
3 B
4 C
5 Hagerly
6 ricky45
7 29 February
8 business
9 conversation/to communicate
10 (at) school

Section 2

11 loyal
12 statue
13 (possibly) count
14 gentle (nature)
15 donations/donors
16 search and rescue
17 (international) database
18 love their food/love food/love eating
19 80 people
20 In a team

Section 3

21 father's workshop
22 1824
23 night writing
24 B
25 A
26 C
27 C
28 mathematics/maths
29 science
30 music

Section 4

31 (particular) events
32 string
33 14 days
34 (a) fortnight/2 weeks/two weeks
35 six months
36 language
37 retrieve/recall/recover
38 (an) argument
39 70%
40 40%

6 ii	This paragraph spells out the dangers of using drugs or resorting to surgery.
7 vi	Research being done on an overweight mouse is significant.
8 viii	… *leptin deficiency turned out to be an extremely rare condition* …
9 metabolism	**Para A**: *obese people have often sought solace in the excuse that they have a slow metabolism*
10 less	**Para A**: *it doesn't matter how little they eat, they gain weight because their bodies break down food and turn it into energy more slowly than those with a so-called normal metabolic rate.* Ref paragraph C also.
11 genetic	**Para D**: *Prof. O'Rahilly's groundbreaking work in Cambridge has proven that obesity can be caused by our genes.*
12 consume	**Para E**: explains that they need to eat *i.e.* consume more than others.
13 behaviour	**Para F**: *Until recently, research and treatment for obesity had concentrated on behaviour modification* …

READING

Passage 1 Tackling Obesity in the Western World

Answers	Location of answer in text
1 x	*However, rather than take responsibility for their weight, obese people have often sought solace in the excuse that they have a slow metabolism* …
2 vii	Dr. Jebb explains that *overweight people actually burn off more energy.*
3 iii	… *researchers were able to show … that her metabolism was not the culprit* …
4 iv	… *Professor Stephen O'Rahilly, goes so far as to say we are on the threshold of a complete change in the way we view not only morbid obesity, but also everyday overweight.*
5 xi	Professor Ian Caterson *is confident that science will, eventually, be able to 'cure' some forms of obesity but the only effective way … to lose weight is a change of diet and an increase in exercise.*

Passage 2 Wheel of Fortune

Answer	Location of answer in text
14 D	*They have the potential both to make the companies in the business a great deal richer, and to sweep them away.*
15 C	*Eventually it will change every aspect of it, from the way cartoons are made to the way films are screened to the way people buy music. That much is clear.*
16 A	*Each such innovation … has been accompanied by a period of **fear** mixed with **exhilaration**.*
17 F	… *the smarter companies in the entertainment business … saw what happened to those of their predecessors who were stuck with one form of distribution.*
18 B	*When the entertainment companies tried out the technology, it worked fine – but not at a price that people were prepared to pay.*
19 C	*What nobody is sure of is how it (the digital revolution) will affect the economics of the business.*

20 F	*Part of the reason why incumbents got pushed aside was that they ... faced a tighter regulatory environment than the present one.*
21 G	*It remains to be seen whether the latest technology will weaken those great companies, or make them stronger than ever.*
22 B	*Old companies always fear new technology. Hollywood was hostile to television, television terrified by the VCR. Go back far enough, points out Hal Valarian.*
23 E	He says, '... *It happened to the oil and automotive businesses earlier this century; now it is happening to the entertainment business'.*
24 C	*MGM, once the roaring lion of Hollywood, has been reduced to a whisper because it is not part of one of the giants.*
25 A	*In 1992, John Malone, chief executive of TCI, an American cable giant, welcomed the '500-channel universe'.*
26 D	This is a reflective piece that looks back at the effects of technological innovation. Hence D is the correct answer.
27 C	The message throughout the text is that technological innovation should be embraced and that resistance does not lead to a positive outcome. Paragraph F in particular asserts this view.

Passage 3 Creative Families

Answer	Location of answer in text
28 IQ/intelligence	**Para 1**: Test(s)/testing percentage definition was *eclipsed by the advent of IQ tests*
29 multi-faceted approach	**Para 2**: *The IQ test has been eclipsed in turn. Most people ... now prefer a broader definition, using a multifaceted approach*
30 B	**Para 4**: *Individual differences were encouraged, and friendly sibling rivalry was not seen as a particular* **problem**
31 C	**Para 6**: *... are often more surrounded by an atmosphere of work and where following a calling appears to be important.*

32 E	**Para 6**: *They may see from their parents that it takes time and dedication to be master of a craft, and so are in less of a hurry to achieve for themselves ...*
33 C	**Para 3**: The conclusion of the experiment was that *a dull rat in a stimulating environment will almost do as well as a bright rat who is bored in a normal one.*
34 A	**Para 4**: *...there always needs to be someone who sets the family career in motion, as in the case of the Sheen acting dynasty.*
35 NOT GIVEN	IQ tests are referred to briefly in the first two paragraphs, but **no information** is given about their reliability. They became less popular amongst researchers.
36 YES	**Para 4**: *This can sometimes cause problems with other siblings ... Their creative talents may be undervalued and so never come to fruition.*
37 YES	**Para 7**: *This last point – luck – is often not mentioned where talent is concerned but plays an undoubted part.*
38 NO	**Para 7**: *Mozart himself simply wanted to create the finest music ever written but did not necessarily view himself as a genius ...*
39 NO	**Para 8**: *Albert Einstein and Bill Gates are two more examples of people whose talents have blossomed by virtue of the times they were living in.*
40 D	The passage discusses how geniuses or very talented people emerge. It considers the factors that have an influence and in particular it focuses on the family environment.

Test 3

LISTENING

Section 1

1   M i t c h e l l
2   66, Women's College/Womens College
3   Education
4   994578ED
5   C
6   B
7   B
8   A
9   C
10   A

Section 2

11 fishing village
12 pine trees
13 marshland/marsh(es)
14 sunbeds and umbrellas
15 longest
16 flag system/flags
17 north(-)west
18 white cliffs
19 sand(-)banks
20 food and drink

Section 3

21 (course) booklists/reading list(s)
22 recommended
23 sales figures
24 year (group)
25 catalogues
26 letters/correspondence
27 inspection/free copies
28 value (for money)
29 clear/easy to use
30 easy to use/clear

Section 4

31 C
32 A/D
33 D/A
34 A
35 B
36 (a) competition(s)
37 design (and) print
38 styles/techniques
39 categories
40 two/2 names

6 A	**Last para**: ... it makes sense to consider the small-scale pollution at home and welcome international debate about this. Scientists investigating indoor pollution will gather next month in Edinburgh at the Indoor Air conference ...
7 C	**Para 1**: ... industrialised countries which encourage a minority of the world's population to squander the majority of its natural resources.
8 D	**Para 2**: ... and left the angry residents wondering how such a disaster could have been allowed to happen.
9 A	**Para 4**: research suggests that it is the process of keeping clean that may be making indoor pollution worse.
10 F	**Para 6**: ... the high-temperature spray, splashing against the crockery and cutlery, results in a nasty plume of toxic chemicals that escapes ...
11 H	**Para 7**: people are so concerned about water-borne pollutants that they drink only bottled water, worldwide sales of which are forecast to reach $72 billion by next year.
12 I	**Para 9**: Overcrowded classrooms whose ventilation systems were designed for smaller numbers of children frequently contain levels of carbon dioxide that would be regarded as unacceptable on board a submarine.
13 G	**Para 9**: 'New car smell' is the result of high levels of toxic chemicals ...

READING

Passage 1 Indoor Pollution

Answer	Location of answer in text
1 D	Short sighted, selfish policies = caused by human self-interest
2 B	**Para 2**: accidentally discharging its cargo into Sydney Harbour ...
3 D	Refer first line paragraph 3.
4 B	**Para 4**: ... baths, showers ... can all be significant sources of indoor pollution
5 C	**Para 8**: ... disproportionate effort is wasted campaigning against certain forms of outdoor pollution, when there is as much ... indoors, right under people's noses.

Passage 2 Robots

Answer	Location of answer in text
14 viii	Paraphrase of first sentence ... whose presence we barely notice but whose creeping ubiquity has removed much human drudgery. Rest of paragraph gives examples.
15 vi	First sentence and ... there are already robot systems that can perform some kinds of brain and bone surgery with submillimeter accuracy – far greater precision than highly skilled physicians can achieve with their hands alone.
16 ix	Final sentence of paragraph C sums up the argument.

17 iv	The paragraph centres on the comparative abilities of robots and the human mind and concludes that: *The most advanced computer systems on Earth can't approach that kind of ability …*
18 i	Some success*: Nonetheless …. they are finding ways to get some lifelike intelligence from robots.* Observing brain functions: *One method renounces the linear, logical structure of conventional electronic circuits in favour of the messy, ad hoc arrangement of a real brain's neurons.*
19 iii	1st sentence of paragraph. Examples of this follow.
20 YES	**Para A**: *Such is the scope of uses envisioned by Karel Capek, the Czech playwright who coined the term 'robot' in 1920 …*
21 NOT GIVEN	The function of Dante is discussed but **no information** is given about whether or not people's lives were saved by the robot.
22 YES	**Para B**: *… there are already robot systems that can perform some kinds of brain and bone surgery with submillimeter accuracy …*
23 NO	**Para C**: The opposite is true: *… when it appeared that transistor circuits and microprocessors might be able to perform in the same way as the human brain by the 21st century, researchers lately have extended their forecasts by decades if not centuries.*
24 NOT GIVEN	The passage discusses robot experiments taking place in Japan but **no information** is given about whether these are the *most advanced* robot systems.
25 video camera	It has *a video camera imbedded in the left eye.*
26 database	*It compares those configurations with a database of standard facial expressions and guesses the emotion.*
27 (tiny/small) pressure pads	*It uses an ensemble of tiny pressure pads to adjust its plastic face*

Passage 3 Saving Language

Answer	Location of answer in text
28 YES	**Para 1**: *But what is happening today is extraordinary, judged by the standards of the past. It is language extinction on a massive scale.*
29 NO	**Para 2**: *In the course of the past two or three decades, linguists all over the world have been gathering comparative data.*
30 YES	**Para 2**: *If they find a language … And we have to draw the same conclusion if a language has less than 100 speakers.*
31 NOT GIVEN	Reasons for language extinction are discussed in paragraph 2. There is **no information** about the relative levels of language extinction in different parts of the world.
32 NO	**Para 3**: Sometimes other considerations are more important: *It is too late to do anything … where the community is too busy just trying to survive to care about their language.*
33 B	**Para 4**: *The community itself must want to save its language. The culture of which it is a part must need to have a respect for minority languages.*
34 D	**Para 5**: *… getting linguists into the field, training local analysts …*
35 F	**Para 5**: *… supporting the community with language resources and teachers, compiling grammars and dictionaries, writing materials for use in schools.*
36 C	*And when the reviving language is associated with a degree of political autonomy, the growth can be especially striking, as shown by Faroese*
37 E	*… new government policies brought fresh attitudes and a positive interest in survival …*
38 B	*… organisations which provide children under five with a domestic setting in which they are intensively exposed to the language.*
39 D	*The solution here was the creation in the 1980s of a unified written language for all these dialects.*
40 F	*This language had been extinct for about a century, but had been quite well documented.*

Test 4

Section 1

1 Sun(day) 2nd July
2 MARINA
3 9.30(am)
4 £1,000/one/a thousand pounds
5 Hong Kong
6 (team) captain
7 parents' permission
8 (20/twenty) life jackets
9 clothes/clothing/set of clothes
10 name

Section 2

11 stamps and coins
12 (shrill) call
13 sense of smell
14 fly
15 introduced animals
16 (scientific) research
17 global education
18 eggs (are) collected
19 chicks (are) reared
20 5% to 85%

Section 3

21 C
22 A
23 A
24 B
25 Sydney
26 Frankfurt
27 A/D
28 D/A
29 B/F
30 F/B

Section 4

31 export/transit {overseas)
32 food shortages
33 lasts longer/lasts much longer
34 food-poisoning/poisoning
35 electricity/electricity supply/supply of electricity/power
36 chemical preservation/add (adding) chemicals/using chemicals (not salt/sugar/vinegar)
37 cheap to store
38 (hot) soup
39 (heated) belt
40 powdered soup/dried soup/dry soup

READING

Passage 1 The Great Australian Fence

Answer	Location of answer in text
1 D	**Para 1**: *To protect their livelihood, the farmers built a wire fence …*
2 B	**Para 2**: *… such a barrier would never be allowed today on ecological grounds.* = people would protest against such a fence being built.
3 C	**Para 3**: *To appreciate this unusual outback monument and to meet the people …*
4 A	**Paras 3** & **4**: He is impressed. He calls it a *monument* and says it is *prodigious* in length.
5 NO	**Para 3**: *It is known by different names but serves one purpose – to form a single dog fence.*
6 YES	**Para 6**: *What is this creature that by itself threatens an entire industry, inflicting several millions of dollars of damage a year despite the presence of the world's most obsessive fence?*
7 NO	**Para 6**: *… the dingo was introduced to Australia more than 3,500 years ago probably with Asian seafarers …*
8 YES	**Para 8**: *It is estimated that since sheep arrived in Australia, dingo numbers have increased a hundredfold.*
9 NOT GIVEN	Text says they commonly represent evil – but there is no information about them attacking humans.
10 YES	**Para 10**: *Now they are ubiquitous for without a native predator the kangaroo population has exploded inside the Fence.*
11 NOT GIVEN	**Para 10**: We are not told what he thinks. He intimates surprise at the number that are killed.
12 B	**Para 7**: *Dingoes officially became outlaws in 1830 when governments placed a bounty on their heads.*
13 A	**Para 10**: *Park officials, who recognise that the fence is to blame, respond to the excess of kangaroos by saying 'The fence is there, and we have to live with it.'*

ANSWER KEY

Passage 2 It's Eco-Logical

Answer	Location of answer in text
14 YES	**Para 1**: *It rapidly became the hottest marketing tag a holiday could carry.*
15 YES	**Para 2**: *There is no doubt the original motives behind the movement were honourable...*
16 NOT GIVEN	**Paras 2 & 3**: discuss the growth of ecotourism but there is **no information** about comparative growth rates.
17 NO	**Para 3**: *Add to this an annual growth rate of around five per cent and the pressure for many operators ... to jump on the accelerating bandwagon is compelling.*
18 NO	**Para 3**: *It is too time-consuming ... many travellers usually take an operator's claims at face value ...*
19 NOT GIVEN	**Para 4**: discusses the questions a potential tourist might ask about an ecotour but provides **no information** on the types of experiences tourists have had.
20 B	**Para 5**: *The society is made up of travel industry, conservation and ecological professionals.*
21 D	**Para 5**: *The society organises something each year. This year it is launching 'Your Travel Choice Makes a Difference', an educational campaign ...*
22 E	**Para 5**: *TES ... has established a register of approved ecotourism operators around the world.*
23 A	**Para 6**: *The scheme is now an independent concern ...*
24 D	**Paras 6 & 7**: Towards the end of paragraph 6 the affiliation of tour operators is discussed. In paragraph 7 it states: *The scheme also allows destination communities to become Green Globe 21 approved.*
25 World Tourism Organisation	**Para 3**: *It is easier to understand ... when we look at its wider role in the world economy. According to World Tourism Organisation figures, ecotourism is worth US$20 billion a year and makes up one-fifth of all international tourism*
26 city entrepreneurs	**Para 4**: NB The question asks **who**. *It is common for city entrepreneurs to own tour companies in country areas, which can mean the money you pay ends up in the city ...*
27 (the) 1992 Earth Summit	**Para 6**: *The Green Globe 21 award is based on the sustainable development standards contained in Agenda 21 from the 1992 Earth Summit ...*

Passage 3 Striking the Right Note

Answer	Location of answer in text
28 ability	First line of text
29 note	First two lines of text explains the ability
30 relative	**Para 2** explains the difference between the 2 skills
31 music lessons	*... may finally settle a decades-old debate about whether absolute pitch depends on melodious genes – or early music lessons.*
32 tone	*... a study that suggests we all have the potential to acquire absolute pitch – and that speakers of tone languages use it every day.*
33 words	They were asked *to read out lists of words*
34 pitch	*... the researches compared the pitches.*
35 cultures	The word *whereas* in the cloze signposts a contrast which appears in the original text as *There's a distinct cultural difference, he says.*
36 D	*... not an all or nothing feature,' says Marvin*
37 B	*Deutsch ... suggests we all have the potential to acquire absolute pitch ...*
38 A	*... the real mystery is why we don't all have absolute pitch, says cognitive psychologist Daniel Levitin.*
39 E	Freimer says: *'There is clearly a familial aggregation of absolute pitch.'*
40 C	Gregerson's studies show that students *with absolute pitch started lessons, on average, when they were five years old.*

Test 5

LISTENING

Section 1

1 692411
2 Rainbow Communications
3 white
4 two/2/boxes
5 light blue (must include 'light')
6 10 packs/10 packets
7 (coloured) floppy disks/computer disks/discs/disks
8 (a/one) wall calendar
9 (a/new) catalogue
10 before 11.30/not after 11.30/by 11.30

Section 2

11 Royal Museum
12 Queen's Park Road/Rd
13 10th Dec(ember)
14 metal work
15 (garden) vegetables
16 coloured stones
17 (white) paper
18 Face to Face
19 pencil drawing
20 all materials

Section 3

21 40 million
22 dogs/the dog
23 only ate plants
24 Polar Bear
25 Brown Bear
26 Sun Bear
27 Giant Panda
28 Sloth Bear
29 B
30 E

Section 4

31 C
32 B
33 C
34 B
35 A
36 C
37 first person
38 (a)new element/helium
39 (the) lost planet/(the) new planet/Vulcan
40 gravity

READING

Passage 1 Twist in the Tale

Answer	Location of answer in text
1 D	She says: Children *have parties – where books are a good present.*
2 A	*'Harry made it OK to be seen on a bus reading a book,'* says Cooling. *'To a child, that is important.'*
3 B	*'Some feted adult writers would kill for the sales,'* says Almond …
4 C	*'Children are demanding readers,'* she says. *'If they don't get it in two pages, they'll drop it.'*
5 D	*It helps that once smitten, children are loyal and even fanatical consumers. Author Jacqueline Wilson says that children spread news of her books like a bushfire.*
6 B	*'People still tell me, "Children don't read nowadays," says David Almond'* … *'The truth is that they are skilled, creative readers.'*
7 A	*'Children's books are going through an incredibly fertile period,'* says Wendy Cooling … *'There's a real buzz around them.'*
8 8–14 years/yrs/ (year-olds)	**Para C**: *The main growth area has been the market for eight to fourteen-year-olds…*
9 Orion	**Para F**: *And advances seem to be growing too: UK publishing outfit Orion recently negotiated a six-figure sum from US company Scholastic for* The Seeing Stone, *a children's novel by Kevin Crossley-Holland …*
10 J.K. Rowling	**Para G**: *After Rowling, Wilson is currently the best-selling children's writer …*
11 D	According to David Almond: … *they ask me very sophisticated questions about use of language, story structure, chapters and dialogue.*
12 H	*But Anne Fine … is concerned that the British literati still ignore children's culture. 'It's considered worthy but boring,'* she says.
13 C	*… there is little doubt that the boom has been fuelled by the bespectacled apprentice Harry Potter…*

14 A	Less than three years ago, doom merchants were predicting that the growth in video games and the rise of the Internet would sound the death knell for children's literature. But contrary to popular myth, children are reading more books than ever.

Passage 2 Fun for the Masses

Answer	Location of answer in text
15 x	1st and last 3 sentences of paragraph.
16 iv	1st sentence of paragraph.
17 i	**Para C**: explains that there were large disparities in the average family income and that … *The share of a family's budget that was spent on having fun rose sharply with its income.* Also it points out that only high earners *could afford such extravagances as theatre and concert performances …*
18 viii	Particularly section commencing: *Moreover, Ms Costa finds that the share of the family budget spent on leisure now rises much less sharply with income than it used to.*
19 ix	*Public investment in sports complexes, parks and golf courses has made leisure cheaper and more accessible. So too has technological innovation…*
20 vi	*By lowering the price of entertainment, technology has improved the standard of living of those in the lower end of the income distribution.*
21 ii	Whole paragraph but in particular 1st and last sentences.
22 F	**Para A**: *Measuring how much people earn is relatively easy, at least compared with measuring how well they live.*
23 G	First mentioned in paragraph C: *The industrial workers surveyed in that year (1888) spent, on average, three-quarters of their incomes on food, shelter and clothing.* Then mentioned again in paragraph D: *By 1991, the average household needed to devote only 38% of its income to the basic necessities, and was able to spend 6% on recreation.*
24 C	**Para E**: *Much of the rest may be due to the fact that poorer Americans have more time off than they used to.*

25 E	**Para G**: *At a time when many economists are pointing accusing fingers at technology … Ms Costa's research gives it a much more egalitarian face.*
26 A	**Para H**: *These findings are not water-tight. Ms Costa's results depend heavily upon what exactly is classed as a recreational expenditure. Reading is an example.*
27 D	**Para I**: She only addresses one issue (C). The strength of the evidence is questioned (A) and there are some flaws (B) but the key sentence is: *Nonetheless, her broad conclusion seems fair.* The rest of the text supports this.

Passage 3 The Art of Healing

Answer	Location of answer in text
28 C	The 1st sentence of paragraph 1 emphasises the sophistication of medicine during the era. The final sentence explains this further: *The organisational context of health and healing was structured to a degree …* i.e. the 'systematic approach'.
29 A	Last sentence of paragraph 3: *They (doctors) were remunerated in accordance with the number of cures they had effected during the past year.*
30 B	**Para 5**: explains that doctors had to meet certain standards when they worked: *The Tang legal code was the first in China to include laws concerned with harmful and heterodox medical practices.*
31 YES	**Para 2**: *… the Tang administration set up … medical colleges with professors, lecturers … to train students in one or all of the four departments of …*
32 NO	**Para 4**: Everyone was encouraged to benefit: *prescriptions from the emperor's formulary were publicised on notice boards at crossroads to enhance the welfare of the population.*

33 NOT GIVEN	**Para 3**: states that citizens were given details of prescriptions but **no information** is given about their lifestyle or influences on it.
34 YES	**Para 5**: ... to treat patients for money without adhering to standard procedures was defined as fraud combined with theft and had to be tried in accordance with the legal statutes on theft.
35 YES	**Para 6**: ... their (texts) contents ranging from purely pragmatic advice to highly sophisticated theoretical considerations.
36 NOT GIVEN	The passage states that the book contained copied formulas but there is **no information** regarding their sources.
37 NO	**Para 7**: The opposite is true: They (sections of Waitai miyao) reflect the Indian origin of much Chinese knowledge on ailments of the eye ...
38 2nd century BC	**Para 7**: continuing a literary tradition documented since the 2nd century BC.
39 prescriptions (and) single substances	**Para 8**: In contrast to developments in the 12th century, physicians relied on prescriptions and single substances to treat their patients' illnesses.
40 Sun Simiao	**Para 9**: Sun Simiao was the first Chinese author known to compose an elaborate medical ethical code.

General Training Module

READING

Part 1 Having a Lovely Time?

Answer	Location of answer in text
1 TRUE	... nearly half said it involved time and effort ... to resolve things.
2 FALSE	The common problems are flight delays, not crowded airports.
3 FALSE	... holiday-makers who complained said it was about the apartment or hotel room
4 TRUE	... it's a credit to tour operators that they [brochures] now contain more detail
5 TRUE	No-one should be palmed off with a poor standard of service...
6 NOT GIVEN	The text does not say this. It simply says you should complain to the right person.
7 TRUE	Take a photo to back up your case.
8 NOT GIVEN	There is no reference in the text to finding someone to write your letter.

Part 1 Hiring a Car Online

Answer	Location of answer in text
9 E	There are photographs of the ... vehicles available.
10 B	There is an inspirational section with detailed directions for some of the great drives ...
11 D	... an extra discount for former clients
12 E	... the whole thing ground to a halt and refused all attempts to access the ... system.
13 C	... you seem to be restricted to cities with airports. ...
14 G	people with older computers may have trouble ...

Part 2 Essay Writing

Answer	Location of answer in text
15 v	**Para A** describes two basic types of essay: creative and analytical essays.
16 iii	**Para C** advises the reader to look carefully at the question i.e. to focus on the task.
17 i	**Para D** discusses ways of collecting background or source material.
18 x	**Para E** talks about writing a plan – this is another way of saying a framework.
19 iv	**Para F** is concerned with the overall production of the essay from introduction to conclusion.
20 vii	**Para G** looks at what to include as support material and to how ensure that it is relevant.
21 two/2	The first paragraph offers **two** ways to approach the assignment i.e. artefact or investigation

Part 2 School of Design

Answer	Location of answer in text
22 a (written) explanation	**2nd para** *You will be expected to provide some … explanation of how and why …*
23 the syllabus document	**Final bullet point** *… and refer to the syllabus document* = read it.
24 a real-life problem	Go to sub heading – Choosing a topic: … *first identify a real-life problem …*
25 work plan backwards	**Last para** *… meet your final deadline* = being on time with your assignment. The text advises that you work backwards when planning.
26 safe	**Last line** *… give due regard to safety and costs.* NB you need an adjective in the answer to match the words 'cost effective' though the text refers to 'safety and costs'.

Part 3 A Stone Age Approach to Exercise

Answer	Location of answer in text
27 C	**Para I**: *Although he is 62, tests showed he had the body of a 32-year-old.*
28 B	**Para 2**: *… cut duration and frequency, and increase intensity.*
29–31 A,C, F	**Para 4**: A = *lots of walking or jogging to find herds …* C *dramatic sprints, jumps and turns etc … walking to sources of water or food, digging … carrying …* F the use of the tense '*this would have meant*' implies the predicability of the activities which he then lists.
32 B	**Para 5**: *Contemporary hunter-gatherers rarely experience the modern killers* i.e. the diseases of developed societies, because they are active. This gives them an 'immunity' to certain fatal illnesses.
33 evolutionary fitness	**Para 3**: He uses the term in paragraph 3 which refers to 'This new science…'
34 order and chaos	**Para 7**: *Exercise should mix order and chaos.*
35 (chronic) aeorobic exercise	**Para 7**: He says this overstrains the heart.
36 weight training	**Para 7**
37 FALSE	**Para 3**: *– life … swung between intense periods of activity and long stretches of inertia.*
38 NOT GIVEN	There is no reference to this in the text.
39 TRUE	**Para 10**: *Our ancestors were adapted to a variety of terrains …*
40 TRUE	**Para 10**: *Human genetic similarity greatly outweighs the variations.*

Sample Answer to Academic Task 1 (page 69)

Band 9 Answer

The three graphs provide an overview of the types of music people purchase in the UK. At first glance we see that classical music is far less popular than pop or rock music.

While slightly more women than men buy pop music, the rock market is dominated by men with 30% buying rock, compared to 18% of women. From the first graph we see that interest in pop music is steady from age 16 to 44 with 20% of the population continuing to buy pop CDs after the age of 45.

The interest in rock music reaches its peak among the 25 to 34 year olds, though it never sells as well as pop. Interest also drops off after the age of 35 with an even sharper fall from age 45 onwards, a pattern which is the opposite to the classical music graph.

Re-states what the graphs show, but in the writer's own words.

Expresses the most obvious of the trends and gives one or two details about Graph 3.

Compares the data in Graphs 1 & 2 describing the overall trends but focusing on 1st graph.

Summarises the data in the 2nd graph by making reference to all three buying populations.

No need for an analysis of the data, suggesting reasons for these buying trends.

Sample Answer to Academic Task 2 (page 70)

Band 9 Answer

In times of high unemployment, employers need do very little to encourage their staff to work hard, but when job vacancies are scarce, they have to find effective ways of rewarding their staff in order to stop them from going elsewhere.

One obvious way of doing this is to offer extra money to employees who are seen to be working exceptionally hard and this is done in companies with a product to sell. For example, real estate agents or department stores can offer a simple commission on all sales.

This style of management favours people who can demonstrate their contribution through sales figures, but does not take into account the work done by people behind the scenes who have little contact with the public. A better approach is for management to offer a bonus to all the staff at the end of the year if the profits are healthy. This, however, does not allow management to target individuals who have genuinely worked harder than others.

Another possibility is to identify excellent staff through incentive schemes such as 'Employee of the Month' or 'Worker of the Week' to make people feel recognised. Such people are usually singled out with the help of clients. Hotels, restaurants and tour operators may also allow staff to accept tips offered by clients who are pleased with the service. However, tipping is a highly unreliable source of money and does not favour everyone.

Basically, employees want to be recognised for their contribution — whether through receiving more money or simply some encouraging words. They also need to feel that their contribution to the whole organisation is worthwhile. Good management recognises this need and responds appropriately.

Introduces the topic and provides a context for the question.

Provides a concrete example and shows the down side of this approach.

Outlines the problems in the first method and suggests a second solution also with a flaw.

Offers another suggestion but also with a potential problem.

Final paragraph addresses the last part of the question and sums up the whole text.

Sample Answer to General Training Writing Task 1

Dear Mr and Mrs. Hooper,

I hope you are all well. The flight home seemed very long but my family all came to meet me at the airport, which was fantastic. Thank you so much for having me — I enjoyed my time with you very much.

I have a favour to ask. When I got home, I realised that I had left a small black handbag in my bedroom. You may recall that I bought myself a new bag while I was in Sydney and I'm pretty sure I put the old one under the bed.

I don't really need the bag but some of the things inside are of sentimental value and I would be very grateful if you could send them to me. There is a red address book, a small leather wallet with some photos and a silver necklace. None of the other things are important so please don't worry about them. Could you please let me know how much the postage is and I will send you the money to cover the cost.

Looking forward to hearing from you soon. Thank you once again for your help.

Love to all the family,

Maria

Informal greeting and acknowledgment of having stayed with them.

States the problem and gives an explanation for her forgetfulness.

Polite request to forward the belongings.

Gives brief description.

Friendly, informal ending.

Sample Answer to General Training Writing Task 2

Band 9 Answer

By comparison with even the recent past, the choice of leisure activities on offer today is vast, so it is reasonable to find that some of these activities reflect the trends and fads of the day.

People have far more money and time than before to pursue their interests but the ever-increasing number of activities does not automatically guarantee continuity. In fact new hobbies come and go. For example, sports such as roller-blading lose their fascination after a few months. Similarly, although snow boarding has taken over from traditional skiing it is doubtful whether its popularity will last. Other things like electronic games go out of date almost as soon as you have bought them because the manufacturers promote the fact that only the latest version is worth having, and so ensure continued sales.

On the other hand, not everyone is a victim of fashion in this way and people of all ages and backgrounds may take up hobbies for social reasons. Traditional hobbies range from participation in active sports like tennis to old favourites such as chess and stamp collecting, and these continue to be popular. By joining a club, people can make friends and feel part of a group with whom they can share a common interest and leisure time. Where sport is concerned, most people know what they like and participate out of love of the game, rather than because it is currently fashionable.

I feel therefore, that while fashion may have an influence, particularly among the young, the majority of people enjoy their hobbies for their own sake.

Addresses the question and partially agrees with the idea.

Develops the argument by giving examples underpinning the 'yes' case.

Puts a strong 'no' case giving the other point of view and supporting it with examples.

Brief concluding paragraph.

TAPESCRIPTS

Skills for IELTS

Extract 1 page 9, Ex 2a

Woman: Good afternoon. Ticket office.
Man: Oh hello! Can we still get tickets for tonight's performance of the concert?
Woman: Yes, there are tickets still available.
Man: How much are they?
Woman: Full price is $35 or $25 concession for students.
Man: $25 sounds OK. And what time does it start?
Woman: Doors open at 6.30p.m. but the concert doesn't begin until 7.15.
Man: Can I get two student concessions for this evening then and collect them at the door?
Woman: Certainly. Do you have your …

Extract 2 page 9, Ex 2a

Man: Good morning. Can I come in?
Woman: Yes. Come on in!
Man: I'd like to enrol for an English course at this college. Can you tell me when the next course starts?
Woman: Right – well the next Intermediate English course begins on Monday 10th September – you could probably join that one – otherwise you'd have to wait until January or April.
Man: I think I'd like to do the next course, if possible. I'm going home in April.
Woman: OK. Could you take a seat and I'll get one of the teachers to have a word with you.

Extract 3 page 9, Ex 2b, page 10, Ex 3b

Man: Oh, good morning. I'm from Rex Research – we're a firm of market researchers and we're doing a survey on shopping choices. Would you mind answering a few quick questions? It won't take a minute.
Woman: Oh! Alright.
Man: Can you tell me whether you wash your hair every day, five times a week, three times a week or less?
Woman: Oh! Usually, every other day.
Man: OK, so let's say ' four times a week?'
Woman: Yes, I suppose so.
Man: Do you always buy the same brand of shampoo?
Woman: Um … I tend to buy a different one each time, I think.
Man: So are you influenced by your budget, the shape of the bottle or the publicity?
Woman: Oh … I think I usually go for value for money – I don't take much notice of the advertising or what the bottle looks like.
Man: Right – thank you for answering our questions. Please accept this free sample with our compliments.
Woman: Oh! Thank you very much!

Extract 4 page 10, Ex 4a, b

1. What I want to emphasise is the cost of the project. Since 1990, £43 million have been spent on the extension to the suburban train line.

2. If you want to get a distinction on this course, you're going to have to put the hard work in. And that means handing your assignments in on time, turning up for all the tutorials and doing well in the exams.

3. It's interesting how some people can be passionate about certain things while others have no interest in them at all. For instance, I have some friends who just love horses. They love to ride them, to breed them and race them. In fact horses are their lives. Personally I can't see the attraction!

4. It was amazing! We were sitting there on the plane in London waiting for the other passengers to board – just about to take off when I looked up and who do you think was coming down the aisle? It was Mike, all the way from Melbourne. And as if that weren't strange enough – he had the seat next to me. I couldn't believe it. What a coincidence!

Extract 5 page 11, Ex 5a

Man: Ladies, gentlemen and children – welcome to the Australian Museum. Great to see so many of you here this morning for the opening of our fantastic exhibition on spiders. As you know, we've got some particularly mean spiders in Australia! But most spiders are quite harmless and play an essential role in maintaining the balance of nature. One of our primary aims with this exhibition is to inform people about these wonderful little eight-legged creatures …

Extract 6 page 11, Ex 5b

Journalist: Can you tell us about the new running shoes which you've developed for the Olympic athletes?
Man: Sure! Well the shoes were designed by a team of researchers at the University of Calgary, where we've been looking at ways of increasing performance by reducing the damaging effects of vibrations on a runner's body.
Journalist: What's so special about them?
Man: Well, basically they can boost the athlete's performance by up to 4%. The shoes are made of conventional materials but by varying the elasticity of the sole, we believe the shoes can slice around four minutes off the time of a marathon runner. Which is the difference between finishing first or twenty-first!
Journalist: Wow!
Man: They may also prove to be useful in helping elderly people to walk, but we're still working on this aspect of the shoe.

Extract 7 — page 11, Ex 6a

Man: Welcome to Portsmouth naval dockyard! We are standing next to what remains of King Henry VIII's ill-fated flagship, the *Mary Rose*. As you may know, the ship sank in July 1545 just off the coast of England not far from here. The king himself apparently watched in horror from the shore, as the sea entered her gun ports, she tipped over and sank to the bottom where she lay for more than 400 years … that's four centuries ... buried in the mud. In 1971 the wreck was re-discovered but it wasn't until 1982 that the ship was raised. Since then a massive research programme has taken place to unravel the mystery of why she sank. One of the scientists is a tree-ring specialist and he's been studying the preserved timbers of the ship and they now believe, after analysing the timbers, they have uncovered a vital clue as to why the ship sank.

Extract 8 — page 11, Ex 6b

Mother: Did the school give you a list of what you'll need for the camping trip?
Daughter: Yes, they did. I've got it here somewhere.
Mother: OK … read it out then.
Daughter: Two pairs of old sports shoes … one woollen pullover.
Mother: Okay, you've got that!
Daughter: One sleeping bag. One foam mattress. No blow-up mattresses allowed as they don't fit in the tent.
Mother: Right.
Daughter: Six pairs of socks.
Mother: Six!
Daughter: Yes.
Mother: And gloves too?
Daughter: No. Gloves aren't on the list.
Mother: And what about a torch for finding your way around in the dark?
Daughter: Yes, flashlight is mentioned and spare batteries too.

Extract 9 — page 11, Ex 8

Student: The new Education building on campus is known as an 'intelligent building'. That means that the lifts are supposed to know if you are waiting for them and the lights should go off automatically if there's no one in the rooms. But in fact, the lights often go off in the middle of lectures and you have to get up and wave your arms around to turn them on again. And in the summer the air conditioning is so cold you often need to wear a coat. I don't think that's very intelligent, do you?

Extract 10 — page 11, Ex 8

Reporter: Over the past 150 years, bicycles have undergone an enormous number of changes. In fact, the bicycle is now a 'mature' product; so much so that any dramatic advances are no longer likely. However, there are still exciting times ahead for the bike. Concerns about pollution, health and traffic congestion, as well as fashion and new construction materials are highlighting the role of the bicycle in our everyday lives and for many people, especially over short distances of less than 8 kilometres, using a bike can often be much faster than driving a car.

IELTS Practice Tests

Test 1 SECTION 1 — pages 30–31

Man: Hello 'Paragliders' Paradise'. How can I help you?
Maria: Oh hi. I'm interested in doing a course in paragliding.
Man: Which course are you interested in?
Maria: Well, I'm not sure. What's available?
Man: Well … we've got the introductory course which lasts for two days.
Maria: OK.
Man: Or there's the 4-day beginners' course which is what most people do first. I'd tend to recommend that one. And there's also the elementary pilot course which takes five to six days depending on conditions.
Maria: We might try the beginner's course. What sort of prices are we looking at?
Man: The introductory is $190; the beginner's course, which is what you'd probably be looking at, is $320 – no, sorry 330 – it's just gone up – and the pilot course is $430.
Maria: Right.
Man: And you also have to become a member of our club so that you're insured. That'll cost you $12 a day. Everyone has to take out insurance, you see.
Maria: Does that cover me if I break a leg?
Man: No, I'm afraid not – it's only 3rd party and covers you against damage to other people or their belongings, but not theft or injury. You would need to take out your own personal accident insurance.
Maria: I see! And what's the best way to get to your place? By public transport or could we come by bike? We're pretty keen cyclists.
Man: It's difficult by public transport although there is a bus from Newcastle; most people get here by car, though, 'cos we're a little off the beaten track. But you could ride here OK. I'll send you a map. Just let me take down a few details. What's your name?
Maria: Maria Gentle.
Man: And your address, Maria?
Maria: Well, I'm a student staying with a family in Newcastle.
Man: So it's care of …
Maria: Care of Mr and Mrs. McDonald.
Man: Like the hamburgers!
Maria: Yes, exactly.
Man: McDonald …
Maria: The post office box address is probably best. It's PO Box 676, Newcastle.
Man: Is there a fax number there, because I could fax you the information?
Maria: Yes, actually, there is. It's 0249 that's for Newcastle and then double seven five four three one.
Man: OK. Now if you decide to do one of our courses, you'll need to book in advance and to pay when you book. How would you be paying?
Maria: By credit card, if that's OK. Do you take Visa?
Man: Yes, fine. We take all major cards, including Visa.

Maria: OK then. Thanks very much.

Maria: Hi, Pauline.

Pauline: Hi, Maria! What's that you're reading?

Maria: Just some information from a paragliding school – it looks really good fun. Do you fancy a go at paragliding?

Pauline: Sure! Do you have to buy lots of equipment and stuff?

Maria: Not really. The school provides the equipment but we'd have to take a few things along.

Pauline: Such as?

Maria: Well it says here. Clothes: wear stout boots, so no sneakers or sandals I suppose, and clothes suitable for an active day in the hills, preferably a long-sleeved t-shirt. That's probably in case you land in the stinging nettles! It also says we should bring a packed lunch. We do not recommend soft drinks or flasks of coffee. Water is really the best thing to drink. We'd also need to bring suntan lotion and something to protect your head from the sun!

Pauline: OK that sounds reasonable. And where would we stay?

Maria: Well look! They seem to operate a campsite too, because it says here that it's only $10 a day to pitch a tent. That'd be fine, wouldn't it? And that way we'd save quite a bit because even a cheap hotel would cost money.

Pauline: Um..or perhaps we could stay in a bed-and-breakfast nearby. It gives a couple of names here we could ring. I think I might prefer that. Hotels and youth hostels would all be miles away from the farm and I don't fancy a caravan.

Maria: No, I agree. But let's take a tent and pray for good weather.

Pauline: OK – let's do it. What about next weekend?

Maria: No, I can't – I'm going on a geography field trip.

Pauline: ….and then it's the weekend before the exams and I really need to study.

Maria: OK, then. Let's make it the one after the exams.

Pauline: Fine – we'll need a break by then. Can you ring and …

Test 1 SECTION 2   page 32

Announcer: The Goodwood Museum is currently celebrating some of the most extravagant types of car design in its festival of speed. Here's our reporter Vincent Freed, who's on site, to tell us about some of the cars on display.

Reporter: Well, here I am, standing in front of one of the most prestigious cars ever built, the Duesenberg, a fantastically expensive, luxurious car built in the early part of the 20th century and bearing all the glamorous qualities of the jazz age. How many were there? Well, only 473 Duesenberg J-types were ever built and the model here is one of the rarest. Each had a short 125-inch chassis or framework and the body was always in the form of an open two-seater. The technology behind the car's 6.9-litre engine was extraordinary. It featured capsules of mercury in the engines to absorb vibration and provide an incredibly smooth ride. In fact, these cars offered unparalleled performance … in an age when 160 kilometres per hour was considered very fast, the Duesenberg promised a top speed of 180 kilometres per hour and could do 140 kilometres per hour in second gear.

Duesenberg, who designed the car, sold it as a frame and engine … this was typical of the age again and many prestige manufacturers such as Rolls-Royce did exactly the same. Owners able to afford the hefty $9,000 price tag for the basic car would then commission a coachwork company to build a body tailored to their own individual requirements.

The Duesenberg's great attraction for the driver, was its instrument panel which offered all the usual features but also several others including a stop-watch. It was the Duesenberg's technology that lay behind its success as a racing car and they dominated the American racing scene in the 1920s winning the Indianapolis Grand Prix in 1924, '25 and '27.

On to another celebrity, the 1922 Leyat Helica. Only 30 of these French propellor cars were built and the model here at Goodwood, which was the fourth to be made, is thought to be the only surviving example still capable of running. The brains behind this car was Marcel Leyat who was an aviation pioneer first and foremost, and the influence of flying is quite apparent in the car. The Leyat very strongly resembles a light aircraft with its front propellor but in this case it's minus any wings of course! It's quite odd to think that this car was whirring through France, just as the Duesenberg was blasting down roads at 160 kilometres per hour across the Atlantic. The Leyats were used regularly in France in the 1920s and were even produced in saloon and van form, as well as two-seater. The Leyat matched its propellor drive with its equally bizarre steering which used the rear rather than the front wheels! But despite looking rather frail, it was a tough machine. In fact, when troops tried to steal it during the Second World War, the car's baffling design was clearly beyond the would-be thieves and it ended up being driven into a tree, breaking the propellor.

And now for the Firebird …

Test 1 SECTION 3   pages 33–34

Tutor: Good morning everyone. Well I think we can start straightaway by getting Rosie and Mike to do their presentation. Would you like to start, Rosie?

Rosie: Yes, well, um, we've done a survey on local entertainment. Basically, we tried to find out how students feel about the entertainment in the town and how much they use it.

Mike: Yes, so we've called our project 'Out and About' …

Tutor: Yes, that's a good title! 'Out and About'.

Rosie: We wanted to find out how well students use the entertainment facilities in town … whether they get to see the latest plays, films … that kind of thing.

Tutor: Now, we have our own facilities on campus of course …

Rosie: Yes, we deliberately omitted those as we really wanted to examine outside entertainment in the town as opposed to on the university campus.

Mike: Actually there were a lot of areas to choose from but in the end we limited ourselves to looking at three general categories: cinema, theatre and music.

Tutor: Right.

Rosie: OK. Well, first of all cinema. In the town, there are three main places where you can see films. There's the new multi-screen cinema complex, the old Park cinema, and a late-night Odeon.

Mike: So if you look at this chart … in terms of audience size, the multi-screen complex accounts for 75% of all cinema seats, the Park Cinema, accounts for 20% of seats and the late-night Odeon has just 5% of seats.

Rosie: As you probably know, the complex and the Park show all the latest films, while the late-night cinema tends to show cult films. So, when we interviewed the students, we thought the complex would be the most popular choice of cinema … but surprisingly it was the late-night Odeon.

Mike: Yeah, and most students said that if they wanted to see a new film, they waited for it to show at the Park because the complex is more expensive and further out of town so you have to pay more to get there as well.

Tutor: Yes, and that adds to the cost, of course, and detracts from the popularity, evidently.

Rosie: Well, next, we looked at theatres. The results here were interesting because, as you know, there's a theatre on campus, which is popular. But there's also the Stage Theatre in town, which is very old and architecturally quite beautiful. And there's the large, modern theatre, the Ashtop, that has recently been built.

Tutor: So you just looked at the two theatres in town?

Mike: Yes. But the thing about the theatres is that there's a whole variety of seat prices. Also, the types of performance vary … so students tend to buy seats at both and like using both for different reasons and if they want cheap seats at the Ashtop, they can just sit further from the front.

Rosie: What we did find that was very interesting is that there are periods during the year when students seem to go to the theatre and periods when they go to the cinema and we really think that's to do with budget. If you look at this graph, you can see that there's a peak around November/December when they go to the theatre more and then a period in April/May when neither is particularly popular and then theatre viewing seems to trail off virtually while the cinema becomes quite popular in June/July.

Tutor: Mmm. I think you're probably right about your conclusions …

Mike: Well, lastly we looked at music. And this time we were really investigating the sort of small music clubs that offer things like folk or specialise in local bands.

Tutor: So not musicals as such …

Mike: That's right.

Rosie: We looked at three small music venues and we examined the quality of the entertainment and venue and

gave a ranking for these: a cross meaning that the quality was poor, a tick meaning it was OK and two ticks for excellent. First of all, The Blues Club, which obviously specialises in blues music. This was a pretty small place and the seating was minimal so we didn't give that a very good rating.

Mike: No! We don't recommend that one really.

Rosie: Then The Sansue which plays a lot of South American music was a big place, very lively, good performers so two ticks for that one. The Pier Hotel is a folk venue … a good place for local and up-and-coming folk artists to play. Not the best of venues as it's in a basement and a bit dark but the quality of the entertainment was reasonable and the lighting was very warm so we felt it deserved an average rating. Finally, there's the Baldrock Café which features big rock bands and is pretty popular with students and we enjoyed ourselves there as well, so top marks for that one.

Tutor: And then did you get any information from the students as to which of the clubs they preferred?

Test 1 SECTION 4

Lecturer: In the last lecture, we looked at the adverse effects of desert dust on global climate. Today we're going to examine more closely what causes dust storms and what other effects they can have. As you know, dust storms have always been a feature of desert climates, but what we want to focus on today is the extent to which human activity is causing them. And it is this trend that I want to look at, because it has wide-ranging implications.

So – what are these human activities? Well, there are two main types that affect the wind erosion process, and thus the frequency of dust storms. There are activities that break up naturally wind-resistant surfaces such as off-road vehicle use and construction and there are those that remove protective vegetation cover from soils, for example, mainly farming and drainage. In many cases the two effects occur simultaneously which adds to the problem.

Let's look at some real examples and see what I'm talking about. Perhaps the best-known example of agricultural impact on desert dust is the creation of the USA's 'dust bowl' in the 1930s. The dramatic rise in the number of dust storms during the latter part of that decade was the result of farmers mismanaging their land. In fact, choking dust storms became so commonplace that the decade became known as the 'Dirty Thirties'.

Researchers observed a similar, but more prolonged, increase in dustiness in West Africa between the 1960s and the 1980s when the frequency of the storms rose to 80 a year and the dust was so thick that visibility was reduced to 1,000 metres. This was a hazard to pilots and road users. In places like Arizona, the most dangerous dust clouds are those generated by dry thunderstorms. Here, this type of storm is so common that the problem inspired officials to develop an alert system to warn people of oncoming thunderstorms. When this dust is deposited it causes all sorts of problems for machine operators. It can penetrate the smallest nooks and crannies and play havoc with the way things operate because most of the dust is made up of quartz which is very hard.

Another example – the concentration of dust originating from the Sahara has risen steadily since the mid-1960s. This increase in wind erosion has coincided with a prolonged drought, which has gripped the Sahara's southern fringe. Drought is commonly associated with an increase in dust-raising activity but it's actually caused by low rainfall which results in vegetation dying off.

One of the foremost examples of modern human-induced environmental degradation is the drying up of the Aral Sea in Central Asia. Its ecological demise dates from the 1950s when intensive irrigation began in the then Central Asian republics of the USSR. This produced a dramatic decline in the volume of water entering the sea from its two major tributaries. In 1960, the Aral Sea was the fourth-largest lake in the world, but since that time it has lost two-thirds of its volume, its surface area has halved and its water level has dropped by more than 216 metres. A knock-on effect of this ecological disaster has been the release of significant new sources of wind-blown material, as the water level has dropped.

And the problems don't stop there. The salinity of the lake has increased so that it is now virtually the same as sea water. This means that the material that is blown from the dry bed of the Aral Sea is highly saline. Scientists believe it is adversely affecting crops around the sea because salts are toxic to plants.

This shows that dust storms have numerous consequences beyond their effects on climate, both for the workings of environmental systems and for people living in drylands …

Test 2 SECTION 1   pages 52–53

Woman: Good morning! University Language Centre. How can I help you?

Man: I'm interested in doing a language course. I did Mandarin last year and now I'd like to do Japanese. Can you give me some information about what courses are available at your centre and when they start. That sort of thing?

Woman: Yes, certainly. Well, we actually offer a number of courses in Japanese at different levels. Are you looking for full time or part time?

Man: Oh! I couldn't manage full time as I work every day but evenings would be fine and certainly preferable to weekends.

Woman: Well, we don't offer courses at the weekend anyway, but let me run through your options. We have a 12-week intensive course three hours three nights a week – that's our crash course! Or an eight month course two nights a week

Man: I think the crash course would suit me best as I'll be leaving for Japan in six months time.

Woman: Are you a beginner?

Man: Not a complete beginner, no!

Woman: Well … we offer the courses at three levels, beginners, lower intermediate and upper intermediate, though we don't always run them all. It depends very much on demand.

Man: I'd probably be at the lower intermediate level – as I did some Japanese at school but that was ages ago.

Woman: Right, well the next Level Two course begins on Monday 12th September – there are still some places on that one – otherwise you'd have to wait until January or March.

Man: No – I'd prefer the next course.

Woman: Right! Can I get some details from you then so I can send you some information?

Man: Sure!

Woman: What's your name? Family name first.

Man: Hagerty. Richard.

Woman: H A G A R T Y?

Man: No, H A G E R T Y

Woman: Oh, OK! And your address, Richard?

Man: Well perhaps you could email it to me.

Woman: Right. What's your email address?

Man: It's ricky45 – that's one word R I C K Y 4 5, at hotmail dot com.

Woman: And I just need some other information for our statistics. This helps us offer the best possible courses and draw up a profile of our students.

Man: Fine!

Woman: What's your date of birth?

Man: I was born on 29th February 1980.

Woman: … 1980! So you're a leap year baby! That's unusual.

Man: Yes – it is!

Woman: … and just one or two other questions for our market research, if you don't mind.

Man: No, that's fine.

Woman: What are your main reasons for studying Japanese? Business, travel or general interest.

Man: My company's sending me to Japan for two years.

Woman: Alright – I'll put down 'Business'. And do you have any specific needs? Will there be an emphasis on written language? For instance, will you need to know how to write business letters, that sort of thing?

Man: No. But I will need to be able to communicate with people on a day-to-day basis.

Woman: OK so I'll put down 'conversation'.

Man: Yes, because I already know something about the writing system at an elementary level and I don't anticipate having to read too much.

Woman: You said you'd studied some Japanese. Where did you study?

Man: Three years at school. Then I gave it up so I've forgotten a fair bit. You know how it is with languages if you don't have the chance to use them.

Woman: Yes, but I'm sure it will all come back to you once you get going again. Now once we receive your enrolment form we'll …

Announcer: Welcome to this week's edition of Country Wide. And today we're taking a look at a number of different breeds of working dogs. And here to report on the dogs with jobs is Kevin Thornhill.

Kevin: Thanks, Joanne. Well yes, dogs with jobs is the subject of today's programme. Dogs have earned themselves a reputation over the centuries for being extremely loyal. And here's a little story which illustrates just how loyal they are. Just outside the country town of Gundagai, is a statue built to commemorate a dog – a dog which sat waiting for his owner to return to the spot where he'd left him. Well … the story, which was immortalised in a song, has it that the poor dog died waiting for his master *'five miles from Gundegai*!', which is where they built the statue. Now that's what I call loyalty!

Well, because of their loyalty and also their ability to learn practical skills dogs can be trained to do a number of very valuable jobs. Perhaps the most well known of working dogs is the border collie sheep dog. Sheep dogs which work in unison with their masters need to be smart and obedient with a natural ability to herd sheep. Some farmers say that their dogs are so smart that they not only herd sheep, they can count them, too!

Another much-loved working dog is the guide dog, trained to work with the blind. Guide dogs, usually Labradors, need to be confident enough to lead their owner through traffic and crowds but they must also be of a gentle nature. It costs a great deal of money to train a dog for this very valuable work but the Guide Dog Associations in the UK, America and Australia receive no government assistance so all the money comes from donations.

Another common breed of work dog is the German shepherd. German shepherds make excellent guard dogs and are also very appropriate as search and rescue dogs working in disaster zones after earthquakes and avalanches. These dogs must be tough and courageous to cope with the arduous conditions of their work. And so that they can be sent anywhere in the world to assist in disaster relief operations, effective dogs and their trainers are now listed on an international database.

When you arrive at an airport here in Australia, you may be greeted in the baggage hall by a detector dog, wearing a little red coat bearing the words 'Quarantine'. These dogs are trained to sniff out fresh fruit as well as meat and even live animals hidden in people's bags. In order to be effective, a good detector dog must have an enormous food drive – in other words they must really love their food. At Sydney airport where there are ten detector dogs working full time, they stop about 80 people a month trying to bring illegal goods into the country. And according to their trainers, they very rarely get it wrong! Another famous working dog is the husky. Huskies, which originally came from Siberia, have been used for decades as a means of transport on snow, particularly in Antarctica where they have played an important role. Huskies are well adapted to harsh conditions and they enjoy working in a team. But the huskies have all left Antarctica now because the International Treaty prohibits their use in the territory as they are not native animals. Many people were sad to see the dogs leave Antarctica as they had been vital to the early expeditions and earned their place in history along with the explorers.

Chairman: We're very pleased to welcome to our special interest group today, Dr. Linda Graycar who is from the City Institute for the Blind. Linda is going to talk to us about the system of writing for the blind known as Braille. Linda, welcome.

Dr. Graycar: Thank you.

Chairman: Now we'd like to keep this session pretty informal, and I know Linda won't mind if members of the group want to ask questions as we go along. Let's start with an obvious one. What is Braille and where does it get its name from?

Dr. Graycar: Well, as you said, Braille is a system of writing used by and for people who cannot see. It gets its name from the man who invented it, the Frenchman Louis Braille who lived in the early 19th century.

Chairman: Was Louis Braille actually blind himself?

Dr. Graycar: Well … he wasn't born blind, but he lost his sight at the age of three as the result of an accident in his father's workshop. Louis Braille then went to Paris to the National Institute for Blind Children and that's where he invented his writing system at the age of only 15 in 1824 while he was at the Institute.

Chairman: But he wasn't the first person to invent a system of touch reading for the blind, was he?

Dr. Graycar: No – another Frenchman had already come up with the idea of printing embossed letters that stood out from the paper but this was very cumbersome and inefficient.

Chairman: Did Louis Braille base his system on this first one?

Dr. Graycar: No, not really. When he first went to Paris he heard about a military system of writing using twelve dots. This was a system invented by an enterprising French army officer and it was known as 'night writing' It wasn't meant for the blind, but rather … for battle communications at night.

Chairman: That must've been fun!

Dr. Graycar: Anyway, Braille took this system as a starting point but instead of using the twelve dots which 'night writing' used, he cut the number of dots in half and developed a six-dot system.

Chairman: Can you give us a little more information about how it works?

Dr. Graycar: Well, it's a system of touch reading which uses an arrangement of raised dots called a cell. Braille numbered the dot positions 1–2–3 downward on the left and 4–5–6 downward on the right. The letters of the alphabet are then formed by using different combinations of these dots.

Student: So is the writing system based on the alphabet with each word being individually spelt out?

Dr. Graycar: Well … it's not quite that simple, I'm afraid! For instance, the first 10 letters of the alphabet are formed using dots 1, 2, 4 and 5. But Braille also has its own short forms for common words. <u>For example, 'b' for the word 'but' and 'h' for 'have'</u> – there are many other contractions like this.

Chairman: <u>So you spell out most words letter by letter, but you use short forms for common words</u>.

Dr. Graycar: Yes. Though, I think that makes it sound a little easier than it actually is!

Chairman: And was it immediately accepted? I mean, did it catch on straight away?

Dr. Graycar: Well, yes and no! It was immediately accepted and used by Braille's fellow students at the school but the system was not officially adopted until 1854, <u>two years after Braille's death</u>. So, <u>official acceptance was slow in coming</u>!

Student: I suppose it works for all languages which use the roman alphabet?

Dr. Graycar: Yes, it does, with adaptations, of course.

Student: Can it be written by hand or do you need a machine to produce Braille?

Dr. Graycar: Well, you can write it by hand on to paper with a device called a slate and stylus but the trick is that <u>you have to write backwards … e.g. from right to left</u> so that then when you turn your sheet over, the dots face upwards and can be read like English from left to right.

Student: Oh, I see.

Dr. Graycar: But these days you'd probably use a Braille-writing machine, which is a lot easier!

Chairman: And, tell us, Linda. Is Braille used in other ways? Other than for reading text?

Dr. Graycar: Yes, indeed. In addition to the literary Braille code, as it's known, which of course includes English and French, there are other codes. For instance, in 1965 <u>they created a form of</u> <u>Braille for Mathematics</u>.

Student: I can't, imagine trying to do maths in Braille!

Dr. Graycar: Yes, that does sound difficult, I agree. And there's also a <u>version for scientific notation</u>. Oh and yes, I almost forgot, there is now a <u>version for music notation as well</u>.

Chairman: Well, thanks, Linda.

Test 2 SECTION 4 pages 56–57

Lecturer: We're going to look today at some experiments that have been done on memory in babies and young children.

Our memories, it's true to say, work very differently depending upon whether we are very old, very young or somewhere in the middle. But when exactly do we start to remember things and how much can we recall?

One of the first questions that we might ask is – do babies have any kind of episodic memory … can they remember particular events? Obviously, we can't ask *them*, so how do we find out?

Well, one experiment that's been used has produced some interesting results. It's quite simple and involves a baby, in its cot, a colourful mobile and a piece of <u>string</u>. It works like this. If you suspend the mobile above the cot and connect the baby's foot to it with the string the mobile will move every time the baby kicks. Now you can allow time for the baby to learn what happens and enjoy the activity. Then you remove the mobile for a time and re-introduce it some time from <u>one to fourteen days</u> later.

If you look at this table of results … at the top two rows … you can see that what is observed shows that two-month-old babies can remember the trick for up to two days and three-month-old babies for up to <u>a fortnight</u>. And although babies trained on one mobile will respond only if you use the familiar mobile, if you train them on a variety of colours and designs, they will happily respond to each one in turn.

Now, looking at the third row on the table, you will see that when they learn to speak, babies as young as 21 months demonstrate an ability to remember events which happened several weeks earlier. And by the time they are two, some children's memories will stretch back over <u>six months</u>, though their recall will be random, with little distinction between key events and trivial ones and very few of these memories, if any, will survive into later life. So we can conclude from this that even very tiny babies are capable of grasping and remembering a concept.

So how is it that young infants can suddenly remember for a considerably longer period of time? Well, one theory accounting for all of this – and this relates to the next question we might ask – is that memory develops with <u>language</u>. Very young children with limited vocabularies are not good at organising their thoughts. Though they may be capable of storing memories, <u>do they have the ability to retrieve them</u>? One expert has suggested an analogy with books on a library shelf. With infants, he says, 'it is as if early books are hard to find because they were acquired before the cataloguing system was developed'.

But even older children forget far more quickly than adults do. In another experiment, several six-year-olds, nine-year-olds and adults were shown a staged incident. In other words, they all watched what they thought was a natural sequence of events. The incident went like this … a lecture which they were listening to was suddenly interrupted by something accidentally overturning, in this case it was a slide projector. To add a third stage and make the recall more demanding, this 'accident' was then followed by <u>an argument</u>. In a memory test the following day, the adults and the nine-year-olds scored an average 70% and the six-year-olds did only slightly worse. In a retest five months later, the pattern was very different. <u>The adults' memory recall hadn't changed</u> but the nine-year-olds' had slipped to less than 60% and the six-year-olds could manage little better than <u>40% recall</u>.

In similar experiments with numbers, digit span is shown to…

Student: Good morning!

Woman: Good morning – can I help you?

Student: Yes, is this where we register for the Beyond 2000 Conference?

Woman: Yes? What's your name and I'll get your conference bag.

Student: Well … I haven't actually registered yet. I was told I'd be able to register today, so I hope that's OK … I've just arrived in Melbourne.

Woman: That should be fine, if you're a student. I'll need to take your details though. So can I have your full name?

Student: Yes, sure. It's Melanie Mitchell.

Woman: Is that M I T C H E double L?

Student: Yes, that's right and that's Ms not Miss.

Woman: OK, fair enough! And what's your address, Melanie?

Student: I live in student accommodation at Sydney University. So my address there is Room 66, Women's College, Newtown.

Woman: OK. And which Faculty are you studying in?

Student: I'm in the Faculty of Education – I'm doing a Master's in Primary School Teaching.

Woman: Right, and may I see your student card because I need to verify that you're a current student?

Student: Yes, sure. Here it is. My number is … 9 9 4 5 7 8 E D.

Woman: OK – now do you want to attend all three days? The conference runs from Thursday to Saturday.

Student: Yes, I think so – if I can afford it. What does it cost?

Woman: Well, you're eligible for a student discount – which makes it $15 for a day registration or $40 for the three days, though it is possible to register for half a day only.

Student: I'll register for all three days, please.

Woman: Good … now will you be requiring accommodation while you're here in Melbourne?

Student: Yes, I suppose I will. What's available?

Woman: Well… we have several levels of accommodation. You can share a room with another student for $25 a night.

Student: Um.

Woman: Or you can have your own room but share the bathroom – I believe it's just down the corridor – that's $45.

Student: Right.

Woman: Or you can have a single room with your own bathroom .

Student: I don't mind sharing a room … On second thoughts, yes I do – I'll have my own room, but I'll share the bathroom.

Woman: Right … Now the conference fee does not include meals though you do get tea and coffee in the breaks. Shall I put you down for lunch – that's an extra $10 a day and there's the conference dinner on Friday night which is $25 … oh, and what about breakfast?

Student: Hang on a minute … it's all starting to sound

rather expensive! I'll have the lunch but not the dinner or breakfast – if that's OK?

Woman: Perfectly OK. Now … a couple of other things – there are a number of special interest groups organised – they're known as SIG's and you're asked to nominate your preference. They'll take place on the Friday afternoon and Saturday morning but they're filling up quickly which is why you need to nominate now.

Student: Right. What are the SIG's?

Woman: Well, there are six altogether. Let's see, on Friday you have a choice between Computers in Education or Teaching Reading Skills…

Student: Um…

Woman: … or a session on Catering for the Gifted Child.

Student: Oh they all sound interesting but technology in the classroom is really my area of interest rather than reading, so I'll go for that. I can probably read up on the gifted child topic myself.

Woman: Right … And then the Saturday options are: a session on Cultural Differences; or there's Music in the Primary Curriculum or you could go to the one on Gender Issues in the Classroom.

Student: Wow! Can I go to them all? They all sound fascinating.

Woman: 'Fraid not.

Student: Well, I am really interested in how boys and girls behave differently, even when they are very young, so I'd better opt for the third session even though the Cultural Differences SIG is probably really interesting, too.

Woman: Right!

Student: … and the Music option would be …

Woman: And how would you like to pay? We accept most credit cards – or bank cheques but not personal cheques, I'm afraid. Been caught out too often before – and cash, of course. We never say 'No' to cash.

Student: I'll have to put it on my card 'cos I don't have enough cash on me, right now.

Woman: That's fine.   Enjoy your time here with us in Melbourne…

Woman: Right, let's move on to the beaches here which are absolutely beautiful. You do have over a hundred to choose from, they're mostly sandy beaches and they vary from the largest which is two and a half kilometres long, to tiny sandy coves. But there are a few that I'd really recommend you to visit.

So looking at this pamphlet, first of all there's Bandela beach. This beach is one kilometre away from the old fishing village of Bandela … which is a beautiful spot. If you park in the car park behind it, there's a small path which leads down to the bay. It's very pretty because the whole beach is backed by pine trees so its very sheltered. The beach itself is very clean and the water is shallow and safe. That together with the soft sand make it an ideal beach for children and non-swimmers.

A little further round the coast, again to the east … in the eastern corner of the island, is the spectacular Da Porlata beach which is basically a long inlet. The land around this beach is marshland … it's all marsh … and there's a stream which winds through it and the stream goes into the sea … and the beach has lovely pale gold sand. Access to this beach is quite tricky and not for the less energetic! You have to go down a long flight of steps – 190 to be exact. But you'll be relieved to know that there's also a road which winds down to a car parking area. When you're level with the sea, there is a handful of shops and bars and you can hire sunbeds and umbrellas.

Continuing round the island, just past the Tip of Caln is the next beach I'd suggest you visit and this is San Gett. Why? Because there isn't a beach longer than this on the island. If you want to know, it's exactly two and a half kilometres long and that's a bonus because it means it never gets overcrowded. It has golden sand and clear, blue water shelving into the sea. There are several beach restaurants to choose from and watersports are available when the water is calm. But check first. This beach operates a flag system as the sea can get rough and you should always swim between the flags. There's a large car park which gives you easy access to the eastern end of the beach but the western end is much quieter and more wild as it is harder to reach.

Blanaka is another popular beach – just in the north-west corner of the island. It has incredibly white sand and sparkling water. There is ample car parking here and plenty of bars and restaurants. Blanaka has white cliffs all around it and for those of you who'd like a little more to do than just lazing on the beach, there are caves here which you can explore in the cliffs and you can also dive into the water from rock platforms along the side of the cove.

Well, my final recommendation for today is Dissidor. Now this beach isn't quite as easy to get to as the others I've talked about. It's quite a remote little beach tucked away here next to Blanaka. You can reach Dissidor by a steep slope which goes over some sandbanks. The beach itself is small and pretty, with reddish-coloured sand and some stony areas on its eastern side. Despite being quite small the bathing is good and you can also go fishing here from the rocks at either side. It's a good idea to take some food and drink with you if you decide to go here as there's only one little bar which isn't always open.

So that should give you plenty of ideas to choose from over the next two weeks …

Test 3 SECTION 3 page 74

Announcer: The start of a new academic year is a challenge for booksellers. Lee Rogers talks to one major book store manager.

Lee: Jenny Farrow, you're the manager of Dalton Books – and you sell an awful lot of books to students, don't you?

Jenny: Yes! We do.

Lee: How do you manage to make sure that you're going to have the books students need when all the new courses begin?

Jenny: Basically, we make preparations long before they arrive. Like all other major book retailers, we have a database of information, and using that, we contact course convenors in May and ask them to send us their booklists.

Lee: How many books are we talking about?

Jenny: For one course?

Lee: Yes, as an example.

Jenny: An average course requires about 30 books. We ask lecturers to indicate whether a book is what we call 'essential' reading … you know, the students simply have to get it … or whether it's what they would term 'recommended' reading or whether it's just a supplementary text that they tend to refer to as 'background' reading.

Lee: What about predicted buyers?

Jenny: It's not a perfect system unfortunately. If a lecturer tells us that he expects us to sell 100 copies of a book, we know that we could actually sell anything from 50 to 150. That's why in practice, when it comes to ordering, it's a lot safer to go by the previous year's sales figures – if that's possible of course … if we've sold the book before. We also build other factors into the equation including the type of course that the books are for, the students' year group and a measure of our own judgement.

Lee: And these criteria make a fairly accurate guide?

Jenny: As accurate as we can be, yes.

Lee: What about the publishers? Do they take an active role in promoting new books?

Jenny: Certainly. The academic and professional publishing market is worth about £700 million a year, so publishers go to some lengths to make sure their books are known. The standard procedure they use is to mail out catalogues to lecturers or colleges and universities, that's been the main form of promotion for years. Now, of course, they can also post details of new or revised works on websites. Some even go so far as writing individual letters to the appropriate lecturers in order to let them know what's coming up.

Lee: The lecturers then contact you if they're interested …

Jenny: That's right. The publishers send us – the book sellers – 'inspection copies'. Lecturers can then get a free copy and decide whether it's going to be suitable for their course.

Lee: And how does it work with the students? What are they looking for and who helps them most?

Jenny: I think lecturers are best placed to understand the students' needs. Often the critical issue is what represents value for money for students. This is more important than price *per se*.

Lee: Do students actually buy books before they start the course?

Jenny: Apparently a large proportion of students wait to see what they need. Students have a firm idea of what constitutes a good book so they tend to give themselves time to look at all the options before making a choice. They tend to go for books that are clear and easy to use. Often the texts that their lecturers recommend turn out to be too academic and remain here on our shelves.

Lee: Well that was Jenny …

Lecturer: I'd like to introduce Rebecca Bramwell, an artist and illustrator, who has come along today to talk to you all about getting your first job or commission as an artist … Over to you Rebecca.

Rebecca: Thank you for inviting me. I remember when I graduated back in 1983, I was very excited about getting my first commission. My degree was in Fine Art and I'd worked long and hard to get it. I was an enthusiastic student and I never found it difficult to find the incentive to paint. I think as a student you're pushed along by fellow students and tutors and the driving force is there. However, when you leave college you find yourself saying things like 'I'll have one more cup of coffee and then I'll sit down to work'. I hate to admit it but I say it myself. Suddenly it isn't finding the inspiration or getting the right paper that's a problem, it's you.

In my view, there are a number of reasons why this happens. It's a real challenge making a decent living as a new artist … you have to find a market for your work, often you work freelance and need to take samples or portfolios of your work from place to place … these experiences are common to a lot of professional people … but artists also have to bare their souls to the world in a way … more than anything they want praise … if people don't like what they create then it can be a very emotional and upsetting experience hearing them say this.

I began to realise that these problems were preventing me from having a career in art and so I decided to experiment. I was a painter but I started to dabble in illustration … drawing pictures for books, cards … and this offered me the opportunity to become more emotionally detached from my work. I was no longer producing images from the heart but developing images for a specifed subject … taking a more practical approach. I began to develop a collection of my illustrations which I put into a portfolio and started to carry around with me to show prospective clients and employers. But it was still tricky because publishers, for example, want to know that your drawings will reproduce well in a book, but without having had any work published, it's hard to prove this.

Having a wonderful portfolio or collection of original artwork is, of course, a first step but what most potential clients would like to see is printed artwork and without this 'evidence' they tend to hold back still when it comes to offering a contract.

Well, I overcame this problem in two ways. And I suppose this is my advice to *you* on preparing your portfolio of your best work. The first way was by submitting my work for a competition, and the one I chose was for a horoscope design and was sponsored by a top women's magazine. There are a few of these competitions each year and they offer new illustrators an opportunity to showcase their work. The other approach I took was to design and print some mock-up pages of a book. In other words, I placed some of my illustrations next to some text in order to demonstrate how my work would look when it was printed.

Perhaps I was lucky in that I had taken a degree that provided me with all-round creative skills so that I could vary my style and wasn't limited to a certain technique. I think that is important. The art world, and many other creative fields, do try to pigeon-hole people into snug boxes with an accompanying label. I think you should try to resist this if you feel it happening to you. If you don't, you'll find it difficult to have new work accepted if you try to develop your style at a later stage in your career. Nevertheless, when you start out and particularly when you're going for an interview, it's important not to confuse people by having a lot of different examples in your portfolio. One remedy for this is to separate your work into distinct categories. In my case, I did this by dividing my design-inspired illustrations from my paintings. It is then easier to analyse the market suited to each portfolio; such as magazines, book jackets, CD covers etc. Working under two names is also useful as it clarifies the different approaches and offers a distinction between them.

I think it's been hard for artists to be recognised in anything other than the pigeon-holes that they have been placed in. Luckily these barriers are slowly being demolished …

Female: Scope charity office, how can I help you?

Male: Oh hello. I'm ringing about the Dragon Boat Race that you're asking people to take part in.

Female: Oh yes, we still need a few more teams. Are you interested in joining the race?

Male: Yes, we want to enter a team but we don't know anything about it? Could I ask you for some more information first?

Female: Of course.

Male: I don't even know when it's being held.

Female: It's taking place on the 2nd July …

Male: Is that a Saturday?

Female: No, it's a Sunday. It's a much more popular day and more people can take part then.

Male: Right. And where's it being held?

Female: … at the Brighton Marina.

Male: Oh, I'm an overseas student … Could you spell that for me?

Female: Yes, it's Brighton Marina, that's MARINA. Do you know where it is?

Male: I'm not sure.

Female: It's a couple of miles past the Palace Pier.

Male: Oh yes, I know it.

Female: You take a right turning off the coast road or you can cycle along the seafront.

Male: That's good. What time does the race start?

Female: Well, the first heats begin at 10.00am – but you need to register half an hour before that – at 9.30 and we really recommend that you aim to be there by 9. It's a good idea to arrange a meeting place for your team.

Male: Right … And the race is to help raise money for charity?

Female: It is. We're asking every team member to try and raise £35 by getting friends and/or relatives to sponsor them. Every crew member will receive a free tournament t-shirt if your team manages to raise £1,000 or more.

Male: Oh that's quite good.

Female: Also we're holding a raffle … every crew member who takes part in the race this season will be entered into a free Prize Draw.

Male: Oh, what's the prize?

Female: It's pretty good – it's a holiday in Hong Kong.

Male: Sounds great.

Female: Is there anything else you need to know?

Male: Could you just tell me a little bit more about the teams?

Female: Well, you need to have a crew of 20 people for your dragon boat … and you then need to agree on who's going to be the team captain … That would probably be you …

Male: Fine. Um, I've got a group of 20 people who are interested … do all the team members have to be a certain age?

Female: Well there's no age limit as such but if you have a team member who's under 18 then they have to get their parents' permission to take part.

Male: Yes, that makes sense.

Female: It isn't dangerous but we do have boats that turn over in the water and for that reason we insist that everyone wears a life jacket as well and you can hire life jackets from us when your team arrives.

Male: What do you advise people to wear?

Female: Well, most people wear a t-shirt, shorts and trainers. I certainly wouldn't recommend that you wear jeans or boots. In fact, it's a very good idea to bring some spare clothes.

Male: OK.

Female: It can get quite cold and wet if the weather's bad. And there's quite a bit of hanging around especially if you qualify for the semi-finals or the final …

Male: I see what you mean.

Female: Have you got a name for your team?

Male: Oh, not yet, no.

Female: Well you need to decide on one and then put it on the entrance form which I'll send you …

Male: Oh OK.

Female: So if you'd like to give me your address …

Test 4 SECTION 2   pages 92–93

Female: Ladies and Gentlemen – welcome to Auckland Zoo on this sunny Sunday afternoon and to our special kiwi fund raising event. My job is to tell you all about the amazing little kiwi – and your job, hopefully, is to dig deep in your pockets.

Now for the benefit of our overseas visitors here today, I should explain first of all that the kiwi is the national bird of New Zealand – and sometimes New Zealanders themselves are known as 'Kiwis'. Now, while kiwis in the wild are a rare sight, the kiwi as a symbol is far more visible. Apart from being in toy stores and airport shops all over the world, you'll find them on our stamps and coins. The kiwi is the smallest member of the genus Apteryx which also includes ostriches and emu. It gets its name from its shrill call which sounds very much like this – *kee-wee kee-wee*. Kiwis live in forests or swamps and feed on insects, worms, snails and berries. It's a nocturnal bird with limited sight and therefore it has to rely on its very keen sense of smell to find food and to sense danger. Its nostrils are actually right on the end of its long beak which is one third of the body length. Now here's an interesting fact. Although kiwis have wings, they serve little purpose because the kiwi is a flightless bird.

Since white settlement of the islands, kiwi numbers have dropped from 12 million to less than 70,000 and our national bird is rapidly becoming an endangered species. This is because they're being threatened by what we call introduced animals animals which were brought to New Zealand such as cats and ferrets which eat kiwi eggs and their chicks.

And so we have launched the Kiwi Recovery Programme; in an all-out effort to save our national bird from extinction. There are three stages to this Programme: Firstly, we have the scientific research stage – this involves research to find out more about what kiwis need to survive in the wild. Then secondly we have the action stage. This is where we go into the field and actually put our knowledge to work – we call this putting science into practice. and then we come to the third stage – the global education stage. By working with schools and groups like yourself, as well as through our award winning kiwi website we are hoping to educate people about the plight of the kiwi.

As part of the action stage, which I just mentioned, we have introduced 'Operation Nest Egg' and this is where your money will be going. It works like this: It's a three-stage process. First of all, we go out to the kiwi's natural habitat and we collect kiwi eggs. This is the tricky part because it can be very difficult to find the eggs. Then, in safe surroundings, away from predators … the chicks are reared. Now this can be done on predator-free islands or in captivity – they're reared until they are about nine months old at which stage the chicks are returned to the wild. So far it's proving successful and since we started the programme some 34 chicks have been successfully raised this year and their chances of survival have increased from 5 to 85%. However, it's not time to celebrate kiwi survival just yet. About 95% of kiwi chicks still don't make it to six months of age without protection. Which is why Operation Nest Egg is so important and we ask you to give generously today.

Test 4 SECTION 3   pages 94–95

Tutor: We're very pleased to welcome Professor Isaac Nebworth to our tutorial group today and he's come to share one of his pet passions with us – City traffic and our western dependence on the motor car. I believe questions are quite welcome throughout.

Professor: Thank you. Well, I know you're all very familiar with the super highway here in Melbourne. But do super highways automatically lead to super wealth, as our politicians would have us believe? I think not.

Tutor: Can you give us an example of what you mean exactly?

Professor: Sure … well, by continuing to encourage this dependence on the motor car, we simply create more congestion and more urban sprawl. And you can see that here in Melbourne right under your nose.

Student: Excuse me. I would just like to say that I feel the sprawl *is* part of the city. The freeways mean people can enjoy the benefits of living away from the centre … on larger blocks with gardens … but still be able to drive back into the city centre for work or entertainment.

Professor: Well I'm not convinced that people want to do that. And is our money being well spent? It may be OK for you now but come back to me in five years' time! Let's take City Link, for example, the new freeway here in Melbourne.

Student: Well … I use the freeway all the time. I think it's great.

Professor: Ah yes, but it cost $2 billion to build, and you could have gotten ten times the value by putting the money into public transport. If you give the automobile road space, it will fill that space … and you'll soon find you'll be crawling along your City Link.

Tutor: But surely, you cannot simply blame the car. Some of the blame must rest with governments and city planners?

Student: Well there is an argument, surely, that building good roads is actually beneficial because most new cars these days are highly efficient – they use far less petrol than in the past and emissions of dangerous gases are low. Old congested roads, on the other hand, encourage traffic to move slowly and it's the stationary cars that cause the pollution and smog … whereas good roads increase traffic speeds and thus the amount of time cars are actually on the roads.

Professor: Well … this is the old argument put forward by the road lobby but, for me it's clear cut. Roads equal cars which equal smog. Public transport is the way to go.

Tutor: Now … on that topic of public transport, I read somewhere recently that Australia isn't doing too badly in the challenge to increase the use of public transport.

Professor: Better than America, granted, but by comparison with Canada, it's not so good. For instance, if you compare Toronto with the US metropolis of Detroit only 160 kilometres away … in Detroit only 1% of passenger travel is by public transport whereas in Toronto it's 24% which is considerably better than Sydney which can only boast 16%.

Tutor: Well I think it's encouraging that our least car-dependent city is actually our largest city. 16% of trips being taken on public transport in Sydney, isn't too bad.

Professor: But it's a long way behind Europe. Take both London and Paris for instance … where 30% of all trips taken are on public transport.

Tutor: Well, they do both have an excellent underground system.

Professor: … and Frankfurt comes in higher still at 32%.

Tutor: I understand that they've been very successful in Copenhagen at ridding the city of the car. Can you tell us anything about that experiment?

Professor: Yes indeed. Copenhagen is a wonderful example of a city that has learnt to live without the motor car. Back in the 1960s they adopted a number of policies designed to draw people back into the city. For instance they paid musicians and artists to perform in the streets. They also built cycle lanes and now 30% of the inhabitants of Copenhagen use a bicycle to go to work. Sydney by comparison can only boast 1% of the population cycling to work.

Student: It could have something to do with all the hills!

Professor: Then they banned cars from many parts of the city and every year 3% of the city parking is removed and by constantly reducing parking they've created public spaces and clean air.

Student: Really!!

Professor: There are also freely available bicycles which you can hire for practically nothing. And of course, they have an excellent public transport system.

Student: Well, that's all very well for Copenhagen. But I'd just like to say that some cities are just too large for a decent public transport system to work well. Particularly in areas with low population, because if there aren't many people using the service then they don't schedule enough buses or trains for that route.

Professor: I accept that there is a vicious circle here but people do need to support the system.

Student: And secondly the whole process takes so long because usually you have to change … you know, from bus to train – that sort of thing, and that can be quite difficult. Ultimately it's much easier to jump in your car. And often it turns out to be cheaper.

Professor: Sure … but cheaper for whom, you or society? We have to work towards the ideal and not give in all the time because things are too difficult … Anyway lets move on to some of the results of the survey … [fade]

Test 4 SECTION 4 — pages 96–97

Lecturer: In today's lecture I'd like to look at the topic of food preservation and start by asking the obvious question 'Why do we need to preserve food?' Well, apart from keeping it fresh for our daily needs, many foods, such as fruit and vegetables are only available at certain times of the year so if we want to be able to eat these foods *all year round*, we need to preserve them. We also need to preserve food for export overseas to make sure that it doesn't perish in transit, and lastly we need to be able to preserve food for when there are food shortages. There are a number of methods of preserving food which involve both high and low temperatures, chemicals, irradiation and drying. Let's have a look at these in turn.

In the 1870s the French scientist, Louis Pasteur, showed that micro-organisms in food could be destroyed by raising the temperature of the food – a process now known as pasteurisation. This involves heating milk to just 65°C for 30 minutes. A new method, the ultra-high temperature or UHT process, involves heating milk to 150°C for three seconds. The advantage of treating milk in this way is that it lasts much longer though I tend to feel, and I'm sure many of you would agree, that taste is somewhat sacrificed in the UHT process.

Tin cans were first used in the early 1800s to store and preserve food. Just as they are now, the cans were tin-plated, steel containers and the process had the advantage of being cost effective. <u>Unfortunately, however, there were many early cases of food-poisoning</u> because the canning process was not fully understood at that stage. We now know the exact temperature and length of time each food needs for proper preservation which has greatly <u>reduced the risk of food-poisoning</u>.

People living in cold climates often preserved food by burying it in the snow and the Romans knew all about the advantages of packing food in ice but for most people this was not an option until the invention of the refrigerator in 1834. Today, however, refrigeration is the most important means of preserving food because the food stays fresh without needing to be treated. However, <u>refrigeration requires an electricity supply</u> and unfortunately if the power goes off, so does the food!!

<u>A variety of chemicals</u> can be added to food and you'll find their names listed on the labels of cans and bottles. Salt is probably the oldest of all <u>the chemical preservatives</u> and was used by many ancient civilisations for many years. Sugar also acts as a preservative and is used to preserve jams in much the same way that vinegar is used to pickle foods. <u>Chemical preservatives are effective</u> but they do not suit all foods and the processes involved are time-consuming.

Another method of preserving food is by drying it. Most foods are 75% to 90% water so if you remove the water the micro-organisms simply can't survive. When food is dried it not only lasts a long time but it also becomes much lighter which is a big advantage as this <u>makes it cheap to store</u>, though some people argue that valuable nutrients are lost in the process. Early methods for drying food involved cutting it into strips and hanging it in the sun or over fires. But there are now a number of more modern methods which involve the use of recent technology. One of these is known as roller drying and it's a highly effective way of making dried foods from liquids, such as soup.

Have a look at this diagram to see how it works. Well, first of all <u>the hot soup is poured</u> in at one end – here. The liquid spreads to form a thin layer <u>on a heated belt</u>. The liquid dries as it moves along. By the time it <u>reaches the end of the belt,</u> all the water has evaporated leaving <u>only dry powder</u>. A blade then scrapes the dried material off the roller and <u>captures it in powder form</u>. All you have to do is add boiling water and you have your hot soup back again, ready to drink!

Another method is called freeze drying …

Test 5 SECTION 1 page 112

Recorded voice: Thank you for calling Millenium Office Supplies. If you would like to place an order, please press one. Your call has been placed in a queue. A customer service operator will be with you shortly.

Woman: Gina speaking. How can I help you?
Man: Oh, hello – I 'd like to order some stationery, please.
Woman: And who am I speaking to?
Man: John Carter.
Woman: Right – can I just confirm your account number and the name of your company, John?
Man: Sure! The account number is <u>6 9 2 4 double 1</u>
Woman: Six nine two four one one. Right, and you're from 'Rainbow Computers?'
Man: No. The company is <u>Rainbow Communications</u>
Woman: Oh, OK, I'll just fix that on the system … <u>comm un ic at ions</u>. And what would you like to order, John?
Man: Envelopes. We need a box of A4 – that is, normal size envelopes
Woman: White, yellow or manilla?
Man: <u>We'll have the plain white please</u> – but the ones with the little windows
Woman: OK … One box – A4 – white – just the one box, was it?
Man: <u>Um. on second thoughts make that two boxes</u>. We go through heaps of envelopes. As a matter of interest. Are they made from recycled paper?
Woman: No. You can't get white recycled paper. The recycled ones are grey and they're more expensive actually.
Man: Right – <u>we'll stick to white then</u>.
Woman: Something else, John?
Man: Yes, we need some coloured photocopy paper. What colours do you have?
Woman: We've got purple, light blue, blue, light green – whatever you want, pretty much. There are 500 sheets to the pack.
Man: Let's see … <u>we're going to need a lot of blue paper</u> for our new price lists so can you give us ten packs, please. Make sure <u>it's the light blue though</u> …
Woman: <u>Ten packs of the light blue</u>. Anything else that we can help you with?
Man: Let me think … what else do we need? I'm sure there was something else.
Woman: Pens, paper clips, fax paper, computer supplies, office furniture?
Man: Oh, yes! <u>We need floppy disks</u> – do you have those <u>nice coloured ones</u>?
Woman: Yes, but they're a bit more expensive than the black ones.
Man: That's alright. I'm not paying, anyway!
Woman: Right. <u>Floppy disks</u>. And what about diaries for next year? We've got them in stock already and it's a good idea to order early.
Man: No – I think we're alright for diaries but something we do need is <u>one of those big wall calendars</u> – you know, one that shows the whole year at a glance. Do you stock those?
Woman: We certainly do.
Man: OK – <u>can you include a wall calendar</u> then, with the other stuff. Just make sure it's got the whole year on the one side.
Woman: Sure – and do you have a copy of our <u>new catalogue</u>?
Man: No, I don't, but could you send one.
Woman: Yes! I'll pop one in with the order. You'll find it a lot easier to remember what you need if you <u>have our</u>

catalogue in front of you next time.

Man: Yes, good idea. And when can you deliver this?

Woman: Should be with you tomorrow morning.

Man: Can you make sure that it's <u>not after 11.30am</u> because I have to go out at 12 there's only myself here on Fridays.

Woman: Fine – I'll make a note on the delivery docket that they should <u>deliver before half past eleven</u>. Thanks very much.

Man: Thanks.

Test 5 SECTION 2 page 113

Announcer: And now for some information on local events and activities. A couple of announcements for art-lovers and budding artists alike. First, a new collection of artwork is going on show to the public next month in the form of an artists' exhibition. The exhibition will include many different types of art … over 100 different pieces, by 58 artists from the local area. <u>It's being held at the Royal Museum</u> which – for those of you who are unfamiliar with the area – is located opposite the library in West Street, right on the corner … <u>the actual address is number 1, Queen's Park Road</u> – it isn't difficult to find. The exhibition will run for 9 weeks and will begin on the 6th of October <u>and continue until the 10th December</u>. So there's plenty of time for you to go along and have a look and I'm sure that will be worth doing.

What will you see there? Well, amongst the items on display will be some exciting pieces of modern jewellery, furniture, ceramics, <u>metal work</u> and sculpture. To give you some examples … Local artist Kate Maine will be there to discuss her collection of pots and bowls <u>that she has made to resemble garden vegetables</u>. They're the sort of thing that would brighten up any dining table, and range from things like yellow cabbage-shaped bowls to round tomato-shaped teapots. Prize-winner Cynthia Course, will also be there to talk about her silver jewellery, all of which she produced using ideas from the rural setting of her country home. Some of her rings are quite extraordinary <u>and have beautiful coloured stones in them</u>. Or if you prefer sculpture, there's plenty of that too. Take, for example, Susan Cup's sculpture of <u>25 pairs of white paper shoes</u>. It sounds easy, but believe me it looks incredible! All of these items along with many others will be on sale throughout the exhibition period.

As part of the exhibition, there will be <u>a series of demonstrations called 'Face to Face'</u> which will take place every Sunday afternoon during the exhibition and these will provide an opportunity for you to meet the artists.

The second set of activities are for those who would prefer to indulge in some artwork themselves … the Artist's Conservatory are holding a series of courses over the autumn period. The courses cover all media and include subjects such as Chinese brush painting, <u>pencil drawing</u> and silk painting. All the tutors are experienced artists, course sizes are kept to a minimum of 15 and there will be plenty of individual assistance.

All the sessions offer excellent value for money and the opportunity to relax in a delightful rural setting. Fees are very reasonable and include the use of an excellent studio and access to the art shop which you will find sells everything from paper to CDs and they also include the <u>provision of all materials</u>. For more information on dates, cost and availability you should get in touch with the programme co-ordinator on 4592 839584 or go direct to the website …

Test 5 SECTION 3 pages 114–115

Interviewer: Alison Sharp has spent much of her life researching bears and in particular bears in danger of extinction. She is the author of a recent book on bears and we welcome her to the studio today.

Alison: Thank you. Delighted to be here.

Interviewer: First of all, can you give us a quick overview of the history of the bear family?

Alison: Well, the bears we know today actually <u>have as their ancestors bears which have been evolving for some 40 million years</u>. We have fossils of the earliest 'true bear' – and it's important to emphasise this because some creatures are called bears but are *not* …

Interviewer: … such as koalas for instance.

Alison: Yes exactly … fossils of the true bear show a small dog-size animal with characteristics that show a <u>blending of dog and bear traits</u>.

Interviewer: So the general belief is that <u>dogs and bears were of the same family</u>?

Alison: Yes, that's the theory. And then we see the arrival of the early Cave Bear. We know from cave drawings that Neanderthal man used to worship this bear and at the same time fear it.

Interviewer: Understandable perhaps …

Alison: Yes, but they need not have worried because the <u>Cave Bear only ate plants</u>. In fact the Cave Bear survived two Ice Ages but then became extinct.

Interviewer: So how many bears can we find today and are any of them in danger of extinction?

Alison: Well I'll answer your first question first. There are eight species of bear in all; among them the American Black Bear and the Brown Bear – from which evolved <u>the newest species of bear – the Polar Bear</u>.

Interviewer: So how old is the Polar Bear?

Alison: Oh, he's a relative newcomer – just 20,000 years old.

Interviewer: And could you tell us a little about them? Which is the largest bear, for instance?

Alison: Well, the largest bear existing today is either the Polar Bear or the Brown Bear.

Interviewer: Right … Don't we know?

Alison: Well, it depends which criteria you use. The Polar Bear *is* the heaviest; the male weighs up to 1,500 pounds but his narrow body actually makes him <u>look smaller than the much more robust Brown Bear</u>.

Interviewer: So the <u>Brown Bear appears the biggest.</u>

Alison: Yes.

Interviewer: And the smallest?

Alison: Well, the <u>Sun Bear is the smallest</u> of the eight species. They only weigh between 60 and 145 pounds.

Interviewer: That makes him a comparative junior!

Alison: Yes. And then next we have the so-called Giant Panda … but that's a small bear too, comparatively speaking.

Interviewer: And are all bears meat eaters?

Alison: No, not at all. In fact the Giant Panda is almost entirely herbivorous living on a diet of 30 types of bamboo.

Interviewer: Oh, yes of course. Panda's are famous for that.

Alison: And another interesting bear is the Sloth Bear which eats insects, particularly termites. He can turn his mouth into a tube and suck the insects out of their nests.

Interviewer: So going back to my second question … Are bears really in danger of extinction?

Alison: Yes indeed … they are … the Sun Bear in particular as they've been hunted almost out of existence. And the habitat of the Panda is also being reduced on a daily basis.

Interviewer: Can anything be done to reduce the threat to these endangered species? I know for instance that it's very hard to breed bears in captivity.

Alison: Yes, well … I think that by raising people's awareness generally we can reduce conflict between humans and animals … to stop the slaughter in parts of the world where bears are still hunted – supposedly in self-defense or to protect livestock, but … often quite unnecessarily. And we can also encourage governments to preserve the natural environment of the bear rather than allow the areas where they live to be systematically destroyed in the name of progress.

Interviewer: Yes, of course.

Alison: And in addition to these global efforts, all profits from the sale of my book will go towards the United Nations Bear Protection program.

Interviewer: That's wonderful … and with the news coming up, thank you for your time, Alison, and best of luck with the book…

Alison: Thank you very much.

Test 5 SECTION 4 — pages 116–117

Male: Good evening and welcome to this month's Observatory Club lecture. I'm Donald Mackie and I'm here to talk to you about the solar eclipse in history.

A thousand years ago, a total eclipse of the sun was a terrifying religious experience – but these days an eclipse is more likely to be viewed as a tourist attraction than as a scientific or spiritual event. People will travel literally miles to be in the right place at the right time – to get the best view of their eclipse.

Well. What exactly causes a solar eclipse – when the world goes dark for a few minutes in the middle of the day? Scientifically speaking, the dark spot itself is easy to explain; it is the shadow of the moon streaking across the earth. This happens every year or two, each time along a different and, to all intents and purposes, a seemingly random piece of the globe.

In the past people often interpreted an eclipse as a danger signal heralding disaster and in fact, the Chinese were so disturbed by these events that they included among their gods one whose job it was to prevent eclipses. But whether or not you are superstitious or take a purely scientific view, our earthly eclipses are special in three ways.

Firstly, there can be no doubt that they are very beautiful. It's as if a deep blue curtain had fallen over the daytime sky as the sun becomes a black void surrounded by the glow of its outer atmosphere.

But beyond this, total eclipses possess a second more compelling beauty in the eyes of us scientists … for they offer a unique opportunity for research. Only during an eclipse can we study the corona and other dim things that are normally lost in the sun's glare.

And thirdly, they are rare. Even though an eclipse of the sun occurs somewhere on earth every year or two, if you sit in your garden and wait, it will take 375 years on average for one to come to you. If the moon were any larger, eclipses would become a monthly bore; if it were smaller, they simply would not be possible.

The ancient Babylonian priests, who spent a fair bit of time staring at the sky, had already noted that there was an 18-year pattern in their recurrence but they didn't have the mathematics to predict an eclipse accurately. It was Edmund Halley, the English astronomer, who knew his maths well enough to predict the return of the comet which, incidentally bears his name, and in 1715 he became the first person to make an accurate eclipse prediction. This brought eclipses firmly into the scientific domain and they have since allowed a number of important scientific discoveries to be made. For instance, in the eclipse of 1868 two scientists, Janssen and Lockyer, were observing the sun's atmosphere and it was these observations that ultimately led to the discovery of a new element. They named the element helium after the Greek god of the sun. This was a major find, because helium turned out to be the most common element in the universe after hydrogen.

Another great triumph involved Mercury … I'll just put that up on the board for you now. See – there's Mercury – the planet closest to the Sun – then Venus, Earth, etc. For centuries, scientists had been unable to understand why Mercury appeared to rotate faster than it should. Some astronomers suggested that there might be an undiscovered planet causing this unusual orbit and even gave it the name 'Vulcan'. During the eclipse of 1878, an American astronomer, James Watson, thought he had spotted this so-called 'lost' planet. But, alas for him, he was later obliged to admit that he had been wrong about Vulcan and withdrew his claim.

Then Albert Einstein came on the scene. Einstein suggested that rather than being wrong about the number of planets, astronomers were actually wrong about gravity. Einstein's theory of relativity – for which he is so famous – disagreed with Newton's law of gravity in just the right way to explain Mercury's odd orbit. He also realised that a definitive test would be possible during the total eclipse of 1919 and this is indeed when his theory was finally proved correct.

So there you have several examples of how eclipses have helped to increase our understanding of the universe, and now let's move on to the social …